Doing Action Research

A Guide for School Support Staff

Claire Taylor, Min Wilkie and Judith Baser

P·C·P

Paul Chapman Publishing

First published 2006

Paul Chapman Publishing
A SAGE Publications Company
1 Oliver's Yard
55 City Road
London EC1Y 1SP

SAGE Publications Inc
2455 Teller Road
Thousand Oaks
California 91320

SAGE Publications India Pvt Ltd
B-42 Panchsheel Enclave
PO Box 4109
New Delhi 110 017

Library of Congress Control Number: **2006904039**

A catalogue record for this book is available from the British Library

ISBN 10 1-4129-1277-6   ISBN 13 978-1-4129-1277-8
ISBN 10 1-4129-1278-4   ISBN 13 978-1-4129-1278-5 (pbk)

Typeset by Pantek Arts Ltd, Maidstone, Kent
Printed in Great Britain by TJ International, Padstow, Cornwall
Printed on paper from sustainable resources

Contents

Claire Taylor is Head of Learning and Teaching at Bishop Grosseteste University College Lincoln and was previously Programme Leader for the Foundation Degree in Educational Studies for Teaching Assistants. **Min Wilkie** is Programme Leader for the Foundation Degree in Educational Studies for Teaching Assistants at the University of Leicester. **Judith Baser** has worked in a wide range of educational settings, including five years as a teaching assistant. More recently, she has run training courses for teaching assistants in ways to support children's learning and development.

Preface

Teaching assistants (TAs) are becoming recognised as professionals with qualifications at higher education level. All these courses embrace research at some point. A method that is pertinent to the marriage between the practical and the theoretical, and is increasingly popular, is action research. This book aims to guide TAs through the research process using the work of some of those who have done it already! Examples are drawn from the work of real TAs who are working in schools and have proved to be successful researchers.

TAs are attaining increasing recognition as professionals by raising their profile through activities such as action research. Part of the process of achieving professional status can also be through gaining recognition as a Higher Level Teaching Assistant (HLTA). To do this, TAs must meet published standards. This book includes activities for reflection which are related to these standards. The intention is to provide a framework within which TAs can explore ideas related to these competencies. It should be made clear that fulfilling the activities will hopefully be good preparation for TAs intending to follow the HLTA route, but will not provide a comprehensive route to meeting the standards without other input.

Exercises, extensions to tasks and other useful information can be found in the appendix section at the back of the book.

Acknowledgements

We would like to thank all the students from the University of Leicester and Bishop Grosseteste University College in Leicester, Lincoln, Peterborough and Stafford who have studied hard since 2001 to gain their foundation degrees. They have shared their experiences and expertise with us, and made incredibly valuable contributions to the lives of children and colleagues in their schools. Particular thanks go to Roy Kirk, Head Librarian at the School of Education, University of Leicester, for all his support, and to the following students who have allowed us to use extracts of their action research projects:

Yasmin Bagworth
Alison Crawshaw
Julie Dowlman
Louise Johnson
Karen Piper
Louise Pointon
Chris Rhodes
Sandra Rycroft
Leanne Sellers
Sue Simmonds
Chris Thomson
Jo Turrell
Louise White

1

Introducing Action Research

Claire Taylor

This chapter will help you to:

- understand the scope of research and why it is important to engage in it
- understand specific terminology relating to research
- investigate the nature of 'action research' and its relevance as a tool for improving teaching and learning
- familiarise yourself with strategies to enhance further development as a reflective practitioner.

What is research?

You are probably reading this book because you have been asked to conduct a research project as part of a school initiative, or a course of further study. If you have not taken part in a formal research project before, you may be feeling a mixture of emotions: daunted, worried, excited, challenged, wondering where to start, overwhelmed. However, have you ever considered that you may already possess some of the skills necessary to engage in worthwhile research?

Education practitioners are engaged in 'research' as part of the routines of day-to-day work in school. Whether it be using the Internet to gather up-to-date resources for a new classroom-based project, observing a pupil to find out why certain behaviours are occurring, or analysing the latest assessments for a cohort of pupils, all of these activities constitute 'research'. Teaching Assistants (TAs) are increasingly at the forefront of such activities and are therefore practising a wide range of research techniques – often without realising it!

Of course, there is a danger, when acknowledging that, potentially, we are all researchers, that an oversimplification of the research process may occur. It is vital that this does not happen. The issues bound up in research are varied, and the complexity of any research task must never be underestimated. It is important, though, to try to define what we mean by research, and in this respect the definition by Bartlett et al. (2001: 39) is helpful in that they describe research as 'the systematic gathering, presenting and analysing of data'. Therefore, research uses the information-gathering practices we all use daily, but in an organised, systematic way, in order to develop theory or deal with practical problems.

Why do research...?

...to improve teaching and learning

Research in schools is becoming an accepted part of professional development, as practitioners seek to gain new insights and understanding of a wide range of school-based issues. Research is attractive as a way to build evidence-based explanations for events and phenomena. As already highlighted above, it implies a systematic approach, built upon order and organisation. More fundamentally, the expectation is for improvements in teaching and learning.

Many 'novice' researchers quickly develop an acute awareness of the direct benefits of engaging in research practice. For example, here are Leanne's reflections upon the importance of research:

> *In the past I have successfully contributed and played an active role in research-based developments within our school, working alongside colleagues, children and parents ... . As a result, I am aware of the positive impact that research can have on future developments and how it informs the raising of standards within a given subject.*

All practitioners have a role to play in improving both standards and the quality of teaching and learning in school. Recent developments in school workforce reform have seen a reconsideration of 'team working', with teaching staff and support staff working collaboratively across the school. Therefore, a whole-team approach to evidence-based research practice has the potential to have a positive and lasting impact upon teaching and learning in a wide variety of educational settings.

...to generate new theory

While focusing on how and why educational practice can be improved is vitally important, it is not the only reason for engaging in research. McNiff and Whitehead (2005) are absolutely clear that action research in particular plays a central part in enabling teachers to be involved in the generation of theory. They go as far as to state that 'teachers are powerful creators of theory and should be recognized as such' (2005: 4). It seems logical to include all classroom practitioners, including TAs, within this statement, if we accept the context of a whole-team approach to evidence-based research practice as informs the raising of standards + quality of l + t

discussed above. Therefore, within the systematic and disciplined approach of a research framework, there are significant opportunities for theory generation as well as for understanding practical processes within teaching and learning.

...to facilitate the development of reflective practitioner skills

In addition to being a useful vehicle through which to spearhead improvement in teaching and learning and to generate theory, the research process is an invaluable tool for the development of reflective practice. The concept of 'reflective practice' within the workplace has been explored by Schon (1983; 1987) and Brockbank et al. (2002); in addition, specific work around reflective practice in educational settings has been explored by Pollard (2002) and others. This theme will be expanded later in the chapter.

Approaches to research

There are many different approaches to conducting research projects, and each methodological approach is situated within a theoretical perspective. Such perspectives may be represented as a continuum. At either end of the continuum are the positivist and interpretivist perspectives, and these in turn align with quantitative or qualitative research approaches, often referred to as 'paradigms'.

Positivism

A positivist approach argues that the properties of the world can be measured through empirical, scientific observation. Any research results will be presented as facts and truths. Of course, the counter argument is that truth is not, and can never be, absolute. A positivist approach generally involves testing a hypothesis, using an experimental group and a control group. In this way, the research is viewed as measurable and objective. However, no research method is perfect and a big drawback of the positivist approach is that the research will not explain 'why'. In addition, statistical correlations do not always equate to causality, and even controlled experiments are not immune to human contamination. However, the positivist approach has brought with it a useful legacy of sound experimental design and an insistence upon quantifiable, empirical enquiry.

Interpretivism

This stance is wholly anti-positivist and argues that the world is interpreted by those engaged with it. The perspective is aligned with a qualitative approach, with researchers concerned to understand individuals' perceptions of the world.

Within this paradigm, researchers acknowledge that there is no single objective reality and that different versions of events are inevitable. Explanations are important and the focus is on natural settings. In addition, the research process is central, with theory developing from data after research has begun, not as the result of a predetermined hypothesis.

With each perspective comes a wealth of terminology and technical jargon, peculiar to the research world. In your reading, you may come across words such as 'quantitative', 'qualitative', 'paradigm' and 'ethnographic', to name but a few. Do not let this specialised language put you off – it has developed to enable professionals within the particular field of research to communicate with each other effectively. Sandra sums this up neatly, in her reflections upon research terminology:

> *Clearly, it is important to get to grips with the language used in research and to be confident that I understand all the meanings.*

Action research sits within the qualitative, interpretivist perspective, but before we consider action research methodology in more depth, it will be worthwhile to summarise some other key styles of research in order to give the bigger, contextual picture of the field of research as a whole.

Experimental research

In this form of positivist, quantitative research, there is usually a hypothesis, which an experiment seeks to prove or disprove. There is an emphasis on reproducing 'lab' conditions in a highly structured way, and on measuring quantifiable outcomes. This approach is heavily reliant on establishing theories of cause and effect.

Case study

This is a useful approach for individuals wishing to research an aspect of a problem or issue in depth. Many education practitioners have conducted case studies investigating particular pupils. The resulting data can be rich and highly descriptive, providing an in-depth picture of a particular event, person or phenomenon. It is the richness of the account that is crucial, and Merriam (1988) is keen to emphasise that case study is more than just a description of a programme, event or process. Rather, case-study methodology is interpretive and evaluative, committed to the 'overwhelming significance of localised experience' (Freebody, 2003: 81).

Ethnography

This style of research was originally developed by anthropologists wishing to study cultural groups or aspects of a society in depth. The approach relies heavily upon observation and, in particular, participant observation. This sometimes demanded complete immersion in the social group that was being studied, in order to fully understand and appreciate the events taking place.

In summary, research projects may be conducted by various different approaches, aligned to certain theoretical perspectives, as shown in Figure 1.1.

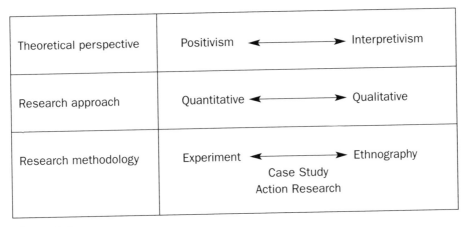

Figure 1.1

What is action research?

'Action research is a powerful tool for change and improvement at the local level' (Cohen et al., 2000: 226).

Essentially, action research is practical, cyclical and problem-solving in nature. Research is seen as a fundamental way in which to effect change. When viewed in this way, the action researcher really is operating at the chalk face and is actively involved in the research process as an 'agent of change' (Gray, 2004: 374).

'Often, action researchers are professional practitioners who use action research methodology as a means of researching into and changing their own professional practice' (Gray, 2004: 392).

The focus for an action-research project is often highly local in nature. Therefore, it is unlikely that research results could be generalised to other settings; rather, the action-research project is concerned with effecting change locally, *in situ*. To this effect, the action-research model has wide-ranging applications and can be carried out by individuals or groups, situated within a class, department, school or cluster of schools. Cohen et al. (2000) suggest an impressive list of possible applications in educational settings, such as changing learning and teaching methods; modifying pupils' behaviour, attitudes and value systems; or increasing administrative efficiency within school. Furthermore, they suggest that action research methodology is useful because it increases professional development, our awareness of the environment in which we work, and our motivation and need for reflection.

The action research cycle

The action research process itself is a cyclical one and was originally developed by Lewin (1946, in Cohen et al., 2000) as a series of steps which included planning, action, observing and evaluating the effects of the action. At first, this can seem a neat, highly ordered view of the process, but it must be remembered that some stages can overlap, and throughout the process runs a thread of reflection on the part of the researcher. However, it is useful to conceptualise the action research process in the following way:

- Identify an area for investigation and a need for change (research).
- Carry out changes (action).
- Look at effects of changes (research).
- Replan/adjust changes (action).
- Repeat!
- *Make a constant effort to link reflection and practice.*

Planning

Getting started on any research project can often be the hardest stage to tackle. The key to success in making a positive start is getting the focus right, and in schools the difficulty may be in prioritising the areas that may make worthwhile action research study material. For TAs engaged in action research, it is crucial that that the area identified for improvement is an area where they can effect change and where they feel motivated to do so. Less successful action-research projects in school have come about as a result of an idea 'given' to the researcher, with the result that interest in the project is lost, ownership of the project is lacking, and action for change rarely happens. In addition, you must be convinced that you have access to the relevant resources and participants. Finally, you should have some idea of what a possible solution could be to the problem. This does not mean that you should generate sophisticated hypotheses related to your action research; you are just trying to imagine the sort of action that could lead to change. If you can answer 'yes' to the questions in Figure 1.2, you may be in a position to start planning your research in more detail.

	Yes	No
Do I consider the issue to be important and does it interest me?		
Do I have the time to bring about change?		
Do I have the resources to tackle this issue?		
Do I have access to relevant participants (pupils, colleagues)?		
Do I have an idea of what a possible action could be that might effect change?		

Figure 1.2

Checklist for choosing an action research focus

If *you* are engaging in action research, *you* are central to the success of the project. In particular, *you* must be able to effect change; therefore, the project must be in an area that *you* can access and work within. The following questions emphasise the central part that *you* will take – notice the prevalence of the pronoun 'I'!

- What do I see as the problem?
- What evidence can I collect to demonstrate that this is a problem?
- What do I see as a possible solution?
- How can I direct/implement the solution?
- How can I evaluate the outcomes?
- What action must I then take?

Acting, observing and reflecting

These areas will be returned to in more detail later in the book, but it is useful to see how the whole action research cycle may operate in practice. When the research focus has been established, the next stage is to decide what sort of actions to initiate and how to capture data related to these actions. Data collection, for example, may involve a range of tools such as interviews, observation, video recording and document analysis. The key principle in choosing data-collection tools is that they must be 'fit for purpose'. This will be discussed more fully in Chapter 3, but, essentially, a data-collection tool will be suitable for the type of evidence to be collected as well as for the type of action being initiated. In addition, due regard must be given to research ethics when carrying out research projects and in particular when gathering data which may be specific to individual participants. This too will be discussed more fully in Chapter 3.

When you have established a research focus and begun to consider methods for data collection, it is strongly advised that at this stage you write a short research proposal, including a timed action plan (see Figure 1.4 for one example). By considering practicalities early in the planning stages, much worry and heartache may be avoided later in the process! The proposal may cover headings such as:

- context – your setting and role
- rationale - why this area for study?
- literature references (a preliminary survey of relevant literature and previous research that may support you in the project)
- proposed action, methodology, practicalities, ethical considerations and thoughts on possible outcomes
- action plan.

Thus, the steps for 'developing a focus' will be as shown in Figure 1.3.

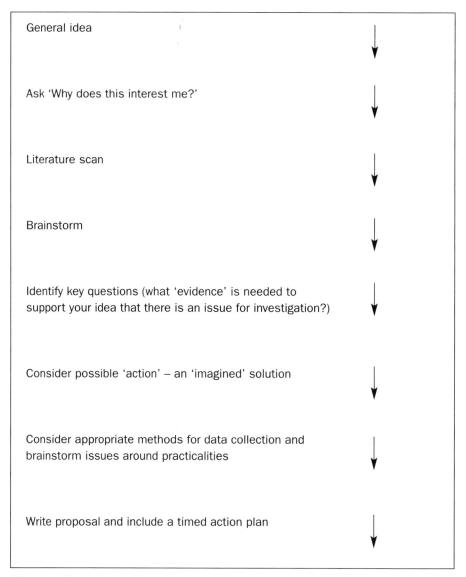

General idea

Ask 'Why does this interest me?'

Literature scan

Brainstorm

Identify key questions (what 'evidence' is needed to
support your idea that there is an issue for investigation?)

Consider possible 'action' – an 'imagined' solution

Consider appropriate methods for data collection and
brainstorm issues around practicalities

Write proposal and include a timed action plan

Figure 1.3

After the action, observation and analysis of its impact will take place, followed
by reflection and evaluation upon the change that has taken place. In this way,
the action research cycle is complete and may be started again, with a view to
refining and repeating the action research processes.

Figure 1.4 shows a sample timed action plan (remember that this is one example only – the exact content and timings will depend upon *you* and *your* project!)

Week	Stage	Activity	Duration	Notes
1	Identification of need and clarification of idea	Literature search	2 days	Access library
2		Investigate video equipment, letter to parents outlining project/asking for permission	3 hours	Check with headteacher
3	Establish starting point	Initial observation to establish issue	20 min	Ensure staff can cover
4		Write proposal Design specific observation schedules/questionnnaires	3 days	Ensure enough are copied
5	Action research cycle 1	Introduce activity to group Conduct daily observations of group Write up observation notes/ analyse/refer to literature Distribute questionnaires	20 min 5 × 10 min 3 hours	Video? Internet search?
6	Action research cycle 2	Adapt initial activity with group Daily observations Write up notes/analyse/ refer to literature Interview headteacher Transcribe interview	20 min 5 × 10 min 3 hours 30 min 3 hours	Video? Tape-record?
7	Action research cycle 3	Activities from cycles 1 and 2 could be further adapted and repeated depending on the data gathered so far – there are no 'rules' as to how many times you complete the cycle of action-reflection-adaptation-repeat.		
8		Collect questionnaires Analyse responses	3 hours	How shall I present the information?
9–12	Evaluation	Continue with additional reading, gather all evidence together, write up research report		

Figure 1.4

Teaching assistants doing action research

Sandra's work supporting a child's physical development

The aim of my study was to support a child who was having difficulties when participating in physical education (PE) sessions. In addition, I wanted to find out if the extra support given, in the form of an additional exercise programme, would have benefits in any other area of the curriculum. I knew that the child I worked with for this study had poor muscular strength and stamina. He found physical activities difficult, whether structured or at break times, his concentration was poor, and he called out at inappropriate times within the classroom. This information had been gathered through evidence such as physiotherapy reports and from my own preliminary observations in school.

Much has been written about the links between physical movement and learning; therefore, the hypothesis for this study was that the child might gain cross-curricular benefits from a structured physical intervention programme.

I have some knowledge and understanding of physiotherapy, as, within my role in school, I work under the guidance of a physiotherapist to deliver specific programmes. This knowledge enabled me to highlight the child in this study as needing some extra support. Discussions with the physiotherapist allowed me to devise a programme of work that would support this child.

Alison's work looking at the impact of visual display within geography

The purpose of my study was to examine the impact that visual display has upon children's learning. It was conducted within the curriculum area of geography, due to the subject's visual nature and also because of restrictions in terms of geography delivery within a very demanding and structured timetable. In the 2000/01 subject report, Ofsted found that there is limited time for geography within the timetable and that it seems to be proving a struggle to get geography valued within schools as a useful and enjoyable subject.

The main concerns that led me to this study were that, despite being recognised as a valuable curriculum subject, geography is timetabled for an hour a week at the most within my workplace, because of the constraints of the core subjects. I was also influenced by a current initiative within my own setting to improve the learning environment and maximise every potential area as a learning tool.

I therefore found value in exploring the concept of delivering some of the curriculum areas by means of visual display. If it could be established that visual display has an impact on children's learning and can be used as an effective learning tool, time could justifiably be spent on its preparation and arrangement. This would not only benefit professional development but also have implications for future use in all areas.

TASK 1.1

HLTA 3.3.8 Organise and manage safely the learning activities, the physical teaching space and the resources for which you have responsibility.

Apply the 'test questions' to Sandra and Alison's studies. How far might these ideas for action research fulfil the criteria for potentially worthwhile projects?

Developing reflective practitioner skills

After she had finished her action research, Alison commented that 'It clarified my position very much as a reflective practitioner, who wants to improve their own practice and develop professionally'.

We have already seen that action research can be a powerful force for change within educational settings. The whole process is practical, pragmatic and concerned with solving problems. Yet there is another dimension, identified clearly by Alison, and that is the opportunity for researchers to reflect upon their own practice and also to reflect upon the research process as a developmental learning process in itself. Thus, the execution of an action research project can bring with it multiple layers and opportunities for reflective practice.

What is reflective practice?

Learning about yourself, and about your own thinking (metacognition), is an important ingredient of any effective learning experience. It is claimed that we do not learn by experience, but by reflecting on experience. By making connections between our experiences, we create meaning and internalise our learning. Some call this 'deep' learning rather than 'surface' learning. Hallmarks of deep and reflective learning include traits such as looking beyond the obvious, challenging the accepted norm and seeking to connect current and previous knowledge, skills and understanding. Engagement in research is often a powerful context through which to engage in such practice.

Recording reflections

One way of developing reflective practice is to articulate your thinking, and this can often be done through a journal or diary. The act of writing can encourage and assist you to become an active learner, by being a reflective learner. In order to do this, you will need to continually think about what you are doing during the course of your action research project, and why and how you are doing it. You may be able to make connections as you write about your project, keeping a balance of retrospection (looking back) and introspection (looking within yourself) in order to participate actively in the learning experience. Such journals can be given all sorts of names, such as 'learning journal' or 'reflective diary', but the key principle is that they provide a vehicle through which to organise your thoughts, feelings, attitudes and hypotheses, as well as to note down practical details related to the project and to make evaluative links to other relevant literature.

Julie describes a learning journal as *having a conversation with yourself and looking back at how your ideas have changed and how your learning has developed*.

There may even be a place for reflective journals within assessed course-work, as described by Pollard:

> ...reflective diaries are sometimes suggested as part of coursework, and might therefore be assessed by mentors or tutors and treated as docu-mentary indications of a trainee's thinking. (2002: 49)

Elliott describes a more practical diary format, linked directly to the project being undertaken, and this format may be developed further and produced in log form:

> It is useful to keep a diary on a continuous basis. It should contain per-sonal accounts of observations, feelings, reactions, interpretations, reflections, hunches, hypotheses, and explanations. Accounts should not merely report the 'bald facts' of the situation, but convey a feeling of what it was like to be there participating in it. Anecdotes; near-verbatim accounts of conversations and verbal exchanges; introspective accounts of one's feelings, attitudes, motives, understandings in reacting to things, events, circumstances; these all help one to reconstruct what it was like at the time. (1991: 77)

Headings may help to structure journal entries, but they are only a guide and must not be seen as a constraint. The journal is *yours* and should be an aid to developing a reflective approach to both study and classroom practice. However, if a structure is helpful, here is a suggestion for key headings that could be used within a reflective journal:

- Date/topic/summary of key points.
- What new learning experience came out of sessions/observations/ classroom experience for me?
- Did I learn effectively? If I did, why? If not, why not?
- What questions have arisen because of today's/this week's/specific event?
- What has interested me? Why?
- What was difficult? Why?
- Have any new ideas/links/issues become clear to me?
- How do my reflections link to what I have read in this field?
- What do I need to think about/find out about/reflect upon next?

Crucially, a key element of any reflective journal must be the inclusion of links to a range of additional literature. By connecting your reflections to other relevant research and theory, you will be able to develop the skills of critical analysis and evaluation, using an evidence base that reaches beyond your own practice.

Teaching assistants keeping learning journals

Leanne – developing a reflective approach to being an action researcher

Entry 1

> *This week's college session provided an insight into strategies that could be used to carry out effective research processes within a school-based project. Within this time, we were introduced to new terminology and structures that would in the future enable us as practitioners to be more analytical and reflective. In the past, I have successfully contributed to and played an active role in research-based developments within our school, working alongside colleagues, children and parents for the benefit of the school as a whole. As a result, I am aware of the positive impact research can have on future developments such as the informed raising of standards within a given subject.*

> *The session included a lot of verbal information. The inclusion of such a vast amount of unfamiliar information in a small amount of time left me feeling anxious. This was a reflection of many influencing factors, including the beginning of a new term, a new module, the unfamiliarity of a given subject, and the way in which the session was delivered, not reinforcing my given learning preference – that of kinaesthetic, experiential learning.*

> *However, after reading the session material, I felt very different. The material provided me with an insight into the process of action research and the benefits it may bring to my work.*

Entry 2

> *Before beginning this entry, I felt it was necessary to read through the previous week's entry. By doing so, I was provided with a brief insight into how I was feeling after the previous week, which could clearly be described as 'very anxious'. It was evident within this time that the use of journal entries was already being identified as a beneficial tool. When we were first introduced to the term 'learning journal', I was not sure what it was, or how it was going to be of any benefit to me.*

I felt a little awkward documenting my fears and anxieties related to the work content and expectations – particularly allowing myself to write down my own fears for others to see and read. However, this is how I currently see the learning journal – helping me to talk to myself and logically think through my anxieties!

Alison – a summative journal entry at the end of an action research project

When I reflect upon the learning that has taken place during this module, I am glad to admit that I feel a sense of achievement and satisfaction from having organised and completed the project task. The process of action research, previously unknown to me, is challenging, frustrating, absorbing, exciting, satisfying and rewarding in a variety of combinations.

The learning which I will take from this experience for use in future projects is the need to avoid developing theories by acting on hunches alone, a statement made by Alan Cooper (1995) in Education Today. *As I developed the project, I became aware of the ease with which we make assumptions about children's learning, without supporting evidence and the impact which this has made upon them. The process of action research requires a level of organisation, open-mindedness and critical analysis that is at times exhausting, but essential to ensure that what we conclude is reasonable and justifiable.*

The skills which I have developed are significant. They have heightened my analytical skills to the point where I am almost reluctant to make a conclusive decision about any aspect of education. My skills of organisation, presentation and interpretation have also developed, and my willingness to discuss and share ideas within the workplace has subsequently increased. As I become increasingly drawn to the theory behind learning, I am able to evaluate other viewpoints and assess them in relation to my own experiences. It has been a valuable learning curve that has enriched my classroom practice, my professional relationship with my peers, and my personal skills and confidence.

TASK 1.2

HLTA 2.1 Be able to acquire further knowledge to contribute effectively and with confidence to the classes in which they are involved.

Search the Internet to investigate how organisations and institutions interpret the terms 'learning journal', and 'reflective diary'.

TASK 1.3

HLTA 2.9 Know a range of strategies to establish a purposeful learning environment.

Spend a few minutes reflecting on what knowledge and skills you have gained from reading this chapter. You could complete a mind map or spider diagram noting down what you know, or you could use the checklist in Figure 1.5 to assess your progress against the chapter objectives.

I understand more about the scope of research and why it is important to engage in it	
I understand some specific terminology related to research	
I know about the nature of action research and its relevance to improving learning and teaching	
I have some strategies for developing my reflective practitioner skills	

Figure 1.5

Key Points

- There are many types of research, but action research is particularly suited to those working in schools or other educational settings.
- It is important to plan your approach and work to an action plan.
- Action research is cyclical in nature.
- Reflective practice makes a good practitioner.

2

Making a Literature Search and Review

Judith Baser

This chapter will help you to:

- understand the purpose and aims of a literature search and review
- develop the skills required to search a range of sources effectively for key information
- develop strategies to analyse and assess sources critically.

What is a literature search and review?

Even though action research ideally focuses on an issue arising out of local circumstances, it is good practice to put the issue into a wider context, enabling you as a researcher to link your findings to the body of knowledge already in existence. To do this, you need to provide evidence of reading and research into the subject area chosen, and show how you have used this to inform and support your work. As Blaxter et al. (2001: 98) point out, it is important 'to engage in related reading' because 'your research project needs to be informed and stimulated by your developing knowledge as you carry it out'.

Education is subject to continuing research, and it is therefore highly likely that whatever you decide to consider for your own project, someone else may already have done some work in that area. There may seem little point in repeating work that has previously been done frequently, effectively and successfully elsewhere, unless you intend to carry it out in some new or different way, or perhaps with an alternative focus, or you intend to replicate work in order to verify findings in your own setting. Once a project focus has been decided upon, the first thing the sensible researcher will do is investigate what work, if any, may already have been done in the area chosen, and what information is available effectively to support and inform the new project. This is referred to as the 'literature search'. This is no longer limited, in these days of ever advancing information technology, simply to material printed on paper (books, journals, documents, magazines, newspapers, etc.), but can now also include the full range of electronic sources available. At the start of the project, when you are beginning to identify the main focus, you need to begin scanning sources, to ensure that there will be a good range of useful, up-to-date background information you can use to underpin your work. Bell advises that

> reading as much as time permits about your topic may give you ideas about approach and methods which had not occurred to you and may also give you ideas about how you might classify and present your own data. (1999: 90)

In this initial scan, you may discover that there seems to be very little supporting literature available. In this case, you might need to consult your tutor, supervisor, mentor or 'critical friend' for some advice and guidance on adapting the terms of your search – for example, to check that you are looking in the right places for appropriate information – or even on adjusting the focus of your project. It may also be that you have managed to choose an area that has genuinely not been the focus of much research. There are probably good reasons for this, which should perhaps be taken as a warning! Blaxter et al. (2001: 125) sensibly suggest that, in this case, 'you should probably consider changing your topic. Ploughing a little-known furrow as a novice researcher is going to be very difficult'.

A major difficulty encountered by new researchers (and by experienced ones, too) is the unbelievable and practically unmanageable amount of information out there! A simple word or phrase typed into an Internet search engine will often produce thousands of 'hits', and when you want only one particular answer, finding the relevant one can be time-consuming and tiring. How do you go about finding the particular material that is going to be relevant and useful to your own particular project, and that is also reasonably accessible to you as a researcher? We will look at ways in which you can refine your search, to make it as effective as possible, later in this chapter.

When you have managed to locate a range of relevant sources of information related to your research topic, your next task is to carry out a literature review. Essentially, this means that the sources you have found need to be examined carefully, and appraised and evaluated, so that you can assess their relevance – and importance – to the project topic.

> A review should provide the reader with a picture, albeit limited in a short project, of the state of knowledge and of major questions in the subject area being investigated. (Bell, 1999: 93)

Once individual research projects have been completed, researchers will write up their findings, and to disseminate these findings to others, they are often first published as reports in academic journals. Research reports are written in a standardised format (see Chapter 5), and near the beginning, after an introduction or sometimes incorporated within it, you will find some para-graphs providing a review of other literature around the project subject area, showing how the current research project relates to the existing body of knowledge.

The more you read, the more you will meet differing opinions, contradic-tions, inconsistencies, bias, disagreements and conflict (often surprisingly vehement, when we tend to think, perhaps a little stereotypically, of research as a rather dry and unemotional subject, supposedly objective and neutral). You need to develop a critical approach to your reading, to consider the con-tent thoughtfully and reflectively, to separate facts from opinions, and to analyse the relevance of all of this to your project work. You can then decide where your own ideas and beliefs fit into the overall picture.

Reading skills

As you begin the literature search, the staggering amount of reading available may now induce a sense of panic; how do you cram all this reading and research into the time you have available? You need to be selective, to make sure that what you choose to read will be informative and useful. There are several things you can do to help yourself cope. The first thing to grasp is that you do not need to read every single word of every source. There are different types or styles of reading you can use to help you find what you want quickly and efficiently.

Scanning

This is the type of reading we all do quite often in our everyday lives – think of looking up a number for a plumber in the telephone directory, or looking up a recipe for chocolate cake in a cookery book. With a clear idea in your mind about exactly what you are looking for, you quickly scan through the informa-tion until you track down the particular items you need. You use information such as your knowledge that directories of businesses list plumbers as a cate-gory alphabetically under *P*, then list all the individual plumbing businesses alphabetically under that heading. You might use extra tricks to choose a reli-able firm to mend your toilet – someone may have recommended a good company to you, or you may be inclined to choose one belonging to a trade organisation that offers some guarantee of professionalism. To find the cake recipe, you can look at the contents list or index of the cookery book to find the appropriate page.

Academic books are generally written in such a way that you can use exactly the same skills and techniques to find the information you need. To start your search, identify a key word, name or phrase, and look for it in either the contents list or the index, which should send you straight to the relevant chapter or page. Scan through the material in the chapter or page by letting your eyes simply wander quickly through what is there, seeking out your key word or words. For tips on common Latin terms used in scholarly writing, see Appendix 2.1.

> **TASK 2.1**
>
> *HLTA 2.9 Know a range of strategies to establish a purposeful learning environment.* Think of some of the key words connected with action research (such as, 'paradigm', 'methodology', 'report'), and try finding text about them by looking them up in the index of this book.

Skimming

This type of reading is used to form an overall idea of the content of a book or article. Read quickly through the material, making use of chapter and sub-headings, content overviews, introductions, first paragraphs in sections, first sentences in paragraphs, and conclusions. You are trying to form an overall impression of what the material is about, rather than understanding every single word.

Reading for meaning

Once you have identified material (through scanning and skimming) that looks as though it will be useful to your research, you need to read it in a much more thorough way, checking carefully as you go along that you have understood the points being made. Before you start, set yourself one or two questions that you hope this source will answer. Making *brief* notes, such as key words and phrases, as you go along might help you to clarify the information you are reading about, although avoid simply copying out large chunks of text, as this will take up a lot of time, without providing any real benefit. Once you have read some text thoroughly, close the book, look at your notes and reflect on what you have learned – have you understood what you have read? Have you found the information you needed, and answers to your questions?

Reading speed

Reading is a skill, just like driving a car or swimming. Practice will help you to improve any skill, and this is also true of reading. As well as being selective about what you read, you can perhaps cram more reading into a limited time by learning how to do it more quickly and efficiently. We generally read by fixing our focus (a fixation) on a word or group of words, then moving our eyes to the right to fix on the next word or group. Rather than trying to increase the actual speed of reading, try to increase the size of the group of words you look at in each fixation; instead of one or two words, look at three or four, or whole phrases. This does take some practice, but with a little application, you can gradually reduce the number of fixations you need for each line, without affecting your ability to take in the information.

The literature search

So, why investigate the literature at all? As Bell (1999) points out, what you read can give you practical ideas and inspiration for the development of your own work, and help you to identify a definite focus, and clarify and refine the topic area, so it is a good idea to try as far as possible to do plenty of your reading at the beginning of the project. Once you have identified a specific subject for your research project, you need to check that you have chosen an area which has a solid body of relevant, recent supporting literature that you can investigate, so research at the start of the project work will help you. Of course, where you look is going to be dictated to a large extent by what the focus is, and it would be impossible to give an exhaustive list. However, some possible starting points are considered in the following paragraphs.

Local resources are a good place to start, so consider those available in your setting, such as school policies and guidelines, information documents for staff and parents, and other people – teaching colleagues (incidentally, newly qualified teachers, who have recently been through the educational process themselves, are often a very useful source of ideas, textbooks to borrow, etc.) including more senior colleagues, such as special educational needs coordinators (SENCOs), senior management team (SMT) members, etc. A good resource is Local Education Authority (LEA) documentation and guidelines and specialist departments and staff (although, at the time of writing, the future of LEAs is unfortunately looking quite uncertain, so they may well cease to exist as a useful source).

Another resource is government documentation – the Department for Education and Skills website contains up-to-date information about the British education system. The **www.dfes.gov.uk** search facility is a good place to start.

Libraries

The library at your own institution is one of the most useful places to begin any search for books, journals, databases, etc. Books are obviously one of the best places to start, but of course they can quickly become outdated. Journals are very useful because they contain material that is current, relating well to what is happening now. Your library will have a good range of these on the shelves, and will probably also subscribe to electronic versions, which you can access through the Internet (from outside as well as inside the institution, as long as you have the relevant passwords and access). The British Education Index (BEI) is, in its own words, a 'database of information about UK literature which supports educational research, policy and practice, alerting interested parties to the existence and availability of useful reading matter' (**www2.dialogatsite.com/atsiteext.dll** at time of writing) and is a useful source for locating information – check whether your library subscribes to it. If you identify a work you would like to look at, but which is not held in your local library, it will usually be possible to arrange access in some way. If it is difficult for you to get to the library, and another university library is closer to you, there is a scheme called UK Libraries Plus. As long as you are a student at a participating library, this allows you to register and use the one closer to you. Your own library can give you any necessary details. It is vital to the success of any academic work that you familiarise yourself thoroughly with the workings of your library – its organisation, cataloguing system, and range of services and how to access them – and particularly its staff of highly trained and well-qualified librarians. It is their job to help you find and access the information you need, so be brave and assertive and simply ask for advice and assistance.

Make sure you practise using the facilities too – there will be induction sessions, but unless you familiarise yourself with the systems and use them regularly, it is easy to forget the details and how to make effective use of them. Memorise any passwords given (or, where possible, change them to something more memorable) or at least, keep a record of them somewhere safe.

TASK 2.2

Try the following exercise to familiarise yourself with your library:

HLTA 2.9 Know a range of strategies to establish a purposeful learning environment.

● Choose a few subject areas (either at random, or connected to an area you are thinking of researching), such as child development, behaviour management, the history curriculum in primary schools – can you find any books, articles or other sources of information on your chosen area?

● Find a textbook with a bibliography. Look through the bibliography and choose a few of the texts listed. Can you find them in your library?

Good sources to investigate may be those recommended by tutors or given in lists of recommended reading. Whenever you read a textbook on a particular subject, have a quick look through the bibliography. You will soon begin to notice that certain names occur regularly, and this is likely to indicate that they are widely regarded as being an important contributor to this area of knowledge, so it might be worth looking for more of their work.

The Internet

As you have surely already discovered, the Internet is a vast source of information, so it can be an important resource for your research. Kirk (2002: 45) identifies a range of Internet resources, such as electronic journals, databases, discussion lists ('communication networks within specific subject areas'), organisations' own websites and search tools ('search engines, subject gateways, Internet guides'). Some of these have already been considered above. You are probably already familiar with Internet search engines such as Google, Yahoo!, Ask Jeeves, or Altavista, which can help you locate information. Subject gateways may be more useful to you, as they scrutinise the material and provide access to reliable sources of information. A very useful one is the Social Sciences Information Gateway (SOSIG) (**www.sosig.ac.uk**), 'a freely available Internet service which aims to provide a trusted source of selected, high quality Internet information for students, academics, researchers and practitioners in the social sciences, business and law' (**www.sosig.ac.uk/about_us/what_is.html** [August

2005]. The content is 'peer-reviewed', that is, it is checked by people with expertise in the subject area, and so can be regarded as reliable. BUBL (**http://bubl.ac.uk**) is a tool used by librarians themselves to access a range of material relevant to many subject areas, including education.

A word of warning, however. It is important to remember that there is no overall organisation of the World Wide Web, and very little regulation or control over the contents of sites. Anybody can post anything, so critical and objective evaluation of Internet material is perhaps more important than for any other sources. All website providers very probably have a particular point of view they wish to put across, so you need to judge the material accordingly. Ask yourself who is providing the information, and why they are providing it. Do they have a particular point of view to promote, or 'axe to grind'? Can you rely on their information to be objective, reliable and unbiased? When was the content first posted, and is it updated regularly?

TASK 2.3

HLTA 2.1 Have sufficient understanding of a specialist area to support pupils' learning, and be able to acquire further knowledge to contribute effectively and with confidence.

Take, for example, the condition known as Attention Deficit Hyperactivity Disorder (ADHD). Look this up on a search engine on the Internet. Choose a selection of the websites that appear and ask yourself the following questions for each of the sites:

● Who has produced the website?

● What is the purpose of the website?

● Is the information given objective and neutral in tone?

● To what extent do you think you can rely on the information given?

What criteria are you using to make judgements?

How to search

Once you have identified the main focus of your research, your next move might usefully be to identify some key words and terms linked to the topic, to make the search for relevant literature a little easier. Use any brainstorming technique you are familiar with (list, spidergram, mind map Buzan [1998], etc.) and jot down as many words or phrases connected with the subject area that you can think of. You might involve a fellow student in this, so that you can both help each other – a little collaborative assistance at this early stage should not be frowned upon, although make sure that the bulk of the project is clearly your own work. For example, if you were going to look at improving playground behaviour in a primary school, you might consider some of the areas shown in Figure 2.1.

Figure 2.1

Each of these areas could be expanded in greater detail, to include alternative terms and expressions as well, depending on the particular focus and aims of your project. The main aim is to give yourself a good range of key words and terms to use in your search for information. These can then be used to search through contents lists and indexes and in search engines on the web. Kirk (in Coleman and Briggs, 2002: 47) recommends putting the 'research topic into one sentence as concisely as possible', as 'not only is this the key to your whole search strategy, but it will also make you think carefully about your topic'. He gives the following example: school *improvement* and the *role* of *middle managers* in *secondary schools*. Kirk suggests finding synonyms (different words with the same or similar meanings) for some of these words and terms, such as 'achievement gains, development, innovation, success' for 'improvement'. This might be helpful in locating a wider range of texts if your initial searches do not seem to be finding very much.

Refining your search using Boolean operators

If your research subject involves using a search engine to find information on a subject on the Internet, and you type in a term, you will usually receive a list of thousands of results, which you then have to go through carefully until you find the particular bit of information you need. You can use Boolean operators to help you reduce the information. These are simple words (named after a nineteenth-century mathematician, George Boole, whose pioneering work on mathematical logic forms the basis of a lot of computer programming principles) which can help you to refine and focus your Internet and electronic catalogue searches. The most simple ones are 'OR', 'AND' and 'NOT', and the SOSIG subject gateway (**www.sosig.ac.uk**) explains quite succinctly how these are used (Figure 2.2).

Search term	SOSIG action
gender AND education	This is the default operator - documents must contain both 'gender' and 'education'.
gender OR education	Documents may contain the terms 'gender' or 'education' - all your terms are relevant.
gender NOT education	Documents containing 'gender' unless they also contain 'education'.
gender education	Documents must contain the phrase 'gender education'.

Figure 2.2

(www.sosig.ac.uk/help/search.html#3simple [August 2005])

Recording information

This is perhaps a suitable juncture at which to mention the importance of recording the sources of information accurately and carefully. An important point to bear in mind is that this time next week, next month, next term, you will *not* remember where you found that incredibly apt, pertinent and totally brilliant quotation! It is never a good idea to rely on memory alone, and there are few things more irritating than having to go back and desperately try to relocate the necessary information. For each source, therefore, while it is still in your possession, you must record all the identifying details you can find about it, such as the author/s, date, full title, publisher/place of publication, and page numbers for direct quotations. Journal articles need the year, volume and issue number, and pages. Internet pages need full Web addresses and date accessed. It is traditional to suggest index cards for this purpose, with a card for each source, so that these can then be filed in whichever way will suit your own particular mode of working. Now, of course, it is more usual to make use of information and communication technology (ICT) resources, and to set up some dedicated files on your PC, and use these in a similar way. There are even bibliographic software systems, such as 'RefWorks', 'EndNote' or 'ProCite', which may be available to you through your library, that will help you to do this job. Use of these electronic systems has the advantage that when writing up the report, you can simply copy any relevant details and paste them into the appropriate place. The actual method chosen is not really important, as long as it works effectively and efficiently for you. There will be more on this, and on the conventions of referring to the work of others, in Chapter 5.

TASK 2.4

HLTA 3.3.6 Be able to guide the work of other adults supporting teaching and learning in the classroom.

Find a willing partner (a fellow student would be ideal). On a visit to a library, each of you chooses a number (say, 5–10) of easily available sources of information relevant to your work, such as books, journals and Websites and notes down as much detail about each source as possible in a list. Arrange a second visit, swap lists and see how quickly you can track down your partner's sources. If you have problems with any of the items, what further information did you need? What was missing?

It is also helpful to spend a few minutes on a brief review of the content of sources consulted along with the details. Jot down notes, bullet lists, key words or phrases, along with some evaluation of the material – was it relevant, useful, informative, surprising, illuminating? Did it support your views and those of others, or contradict them? Did you agree with the author's views and ideas, or perhaps feel that they were not borne out by your own experiences? Notes such as these made at the time of reading, when the material is still fresh in your mind, will be very helpful when you write the literature review section of the project report.

The literature review

Having spent a considerable number of hours reading through material, you need to show how you are going to make good use of all this background investigation for a solid basis for your own work. When you write your project report (see Chapter 5), there will be a section in which you examine your sources, consider the content, reflect on it and appraise it critically. The word 'critical' in this context does not simply mean finding fault; it is more a case of assessing what you have read, thinking about it and evaluating your response to it, as well as comparing different views and responses. After finishing reading a text, ask yourself some basic questions about it. What have you learned from reading this? Support for a point of view already held? Something new, which you had previously never thought of? An idea that contradicts what you previously thought? Do you agree with what the writer has said?

Thus, your review of your reading is meant to be a critical review – a thoughtful and carefully considered appraisal and evaluation of your reading and research. It is a good idea to try to avoid what Haywood and Wragg call

the *uncritical* review, the furniture sale catalogue, in which everything merits a one paragraph entry … Bloggs (1975) found this, Smith (1976) found that, Jones (1977) found the other, Bloggs, Smith and Jones (1978) found happiness in heaven. (1978: 2)

Most tutors are delighted when a student demonstrates a little independent thinking. The fact that something has been printed in a book does not mean that you have to agree with it, particularly if your own experience or findings, or more extensive research seems to contradict it. If you can justify your own opinion, idea or point of view, do not be afraid to express it!

To give you some idea of how a literature review might look, here are some examples. Below are some extracts from Karen's literature review. Her project investigated the effects of introducing traditional playground games in a primary school setting, in an attempt to improve behaviour at playtimes and lunchtimes.

Extracts from Karen's literature review

A focused search on ERIC revealed scant literature on the research topic. Much of that reviewed was based around the theme of health and safety. A number of articles and newspaper reports outlined the difficulties faced by schools when allowing children to play physical games in the playground. As a result, according to Kirkman (2000), 'over-protective school staff are in danger of taking all the fun and spontaneity out of playtimes'. Many games are now banned, such as British bulldog, tag, and stuck in the mud. Thomson (cited by Allirajah, 2001) states that skipping is banned in some schools, as children tie their legs together for three-legged races or trip on the ropes. Football has met the same demise, although Blatchford et al. (2003) reported that ball games led to positive behaviour among children.

Recent news reports have questioned the need for wearing goggles while playing conkers, while some schools ban conkers, referring to them as 'lethal weapons' (Thomson, cited by Kirkman, 2000). Thomson concludes that 'excessive restraints are being placed on play'. The Labour Party manifesto promised a 'sports entitlement for all children, giving them access to at least two hours of sport in or after school' (Allirajah, 2001); this is, however, being undermined by schools banning playground games.

Literature from the British Heart Foundation (BHF, 2001) cites the Health Education Authority (HEA, 1998) in saying that their daily recommended time for physical activity (one hour) is met in part by the playground break time. They recommend therefore that schools should introduce a whole-school approach, encouraging rather than banning active playtimes. The BHF (2001) also highlight that failure to allow this type of play deprives children of the experience of working out their own rules for behaviour. They state that this could lead to a lack of confidence in adults in decision-making and difficulty in forming friendships. The BHF (2001), along with McGregor (2004), report that organised play can reduce bullying by offering social experiences rather than competitive ones. This is reiterated by Dike (1999), who says that 'if you give a dominant child something new to learn, they have to relate to other children and learn to share and co-operate'.

The Ingenta search engine enables access to published work on various aspects of playground activity. These are mostly based on the themes of children's development, gender and ethnic differences, aggression and, generally, the importance of play as a tool for social and cognitive learning. A search on the McGraw-Hill website revealed a useful text by Bishop and Curtis (2005) on the history of playground games and the relevance of these game values in today's society, but offered little in relation to health and safety considerations. The above literature review, along with my experiences, helped to generate the research problem and question.

Karen has thus provided a summary of her main findings from her investigative research, and in her report, she goes on to provide a brief account of how she developed her project, which arose out of a series of incidents she observed when on playground duty, and also (as mentioned in the literature review) through reading about incidents in the news media.

Sue works with Key Stage 3 students who need learning support and she decided to investigate the use of Tony Buzan's 'mind maps' in her work. Her work is also mentioned in Chapter 4. She provided some thoughtful and critical consideration of her chosen subject area, linking it effectively to learning done earlier in the course – see below for examples from her literature review.

Extracts from Sue's literature review

Smith (2003) referred to mind mapping in conjunction with Gardner's Theory of Multiple Intelligences, which identified the need for learning through a number of routes, such as music and movement. It was difficult to see how mind maps would accommodate the needs of such kinaesthetic learners, who preferred action to stasis, but Smith advocated offering the strategy as one of a range of options, whereas Buzan seemed to offer it as the only option … .

Hughes (1999: 41) acknowledged the fact the learners do have preferred learning styles, but said, 'These … are preferences and do not mean that the individual can only learn in one way … however, people learn most effectively when working in their preferred styles'. This made me wonder whether some children would, despite responding positively to mind maps, still say that they preferred to learn in other ways. Moreover, it seemed highly unlikely that everyone would like them. It would be interesting to assess the extent to which mind maps, through individual accommodation and adaptation, would facilitate learning needs. Consultation of previous modules ... made me examine the extent to which Buzan had not taken other learning requirements into consideration, such as social interaction (Vygotsky, 1924).

Another consideration for my research was whether there would be a gender issue in the reaction to mind maps, and I consulted Dwyer and Charles (2003), and Jarvis et al. (2001) for further information. Influenced by this ... I decided to investigate further, because I felt that there was the potential for boys and girls to view the mind map concept differently.

Further background research was carried out with ICT software, such as Inspiration *and* MindManager, *but I discounted the use of these methods because they proved to be too time-consuming and they required a good standard of ICT skills, not only from the pupils, but also from the teacher!*

Sue has not simply accepted Buzan's ideas, but has obviously given them a lot of careful thought, and has been prepared to appraise them with a critical attitude.

Research and reading can be very time-consuming, but a certain amount is inevitable if you are to show how your own project links to work already done, to accepted practice, and to current thinking. Even so, you may need to recognise that you will reach a point when you need to limit your background research efforts and focus on the actual project work. Blaxter et al. advise:

You should try to get a good understanding of the literature as early as you can in your research, aiming to appreciate the breadth of the literature and to understand in more depth the specific parts of it of most relevance to you. You should then move on to the actual research itself, but keep up with and return to reading to refresh, check and update yourself when you can. (2001: 127)

Key Points

- It is necessary to demonstrate an awareness of the perspectives of others with respect to your chosen subject matter.
- Ask for advice from those around you – sharing ideas can be very fruitful!
- It is worthwhile developing your skills in a variety of search methods.
- Good planning and research are critical to a well-balanced project.

Gathering Data

Claire Taylor

This chapter will help you to:

- understand the range of methods available for collecting research data
- evaluate the appropriateness and effectiveness of different data collection methods
- consider the practicalities involved in collecting research data
- consider ethical issues related to data collection.

After you have decided on the focus of your action research project, the next stage is to consider what data, or information, you may need. Various stages of the project will require information to be gathered. For example, you may need to gather information at the very start of the project – to identify your research area, as part of a diagnostic process, or to establish exactly what your starting point is. In an action research project, information will be gathered during the action research cycle. This will then be analysed and the results used to inform the next stage of the action. Regardless of when your information is gathered, the key question is, 'What do I need to know?' Once you have an answer to this question, you can start to consider how best to gather the information.

Which method?

There are many factors that may influence the choice of data collection methods. A key aspect to consider is *fitness for purpose*. In other words, does the method capture the information you are looking for? There may also be very practical and ethical considerations about which method to use. These could include time, cost and problems of access. In addition, it is essential to assess the extent to which forms of data collection are reliable and valid.

Reliability

'Reliability is the extent to which a test or procedure produces similar results under constant conditions on all occasions' (Bell, 1999: 103). In other words, for a data-collection method to be reliable, we would expect it to give us the same results whether something was measured today, yesterday or tomorrow. However, this does rely upon the fact that the underlying aspects being measured have not changed, and often with qualitative research that cannot be guaranteed. For example, you may wish to collect data related to behaviour in the classroom, such as information about specific actions, but these actions may be influenced by all sorts of other factors, including individuals, changes in the environment, interpersonal dynamics, etc. Therefore, it is important to be clear about what you are measuring, or 'what I need to know', in order to assess the reliability of a data-collection tool and the extent of the variables that may affect your research.

Validity

Validity is a little more complex than reliability in that it tells us whether a data-collection tool actually measures or collects the information it was intended to. For example, a researcher may ask questions which are reliable, but they may not be valid in terms of the information that is sought. Gray (2004) gives the example posed by McBurney (1998), who suggested that a measure of someone's hat size might determine intelligence. You could measure the hat size on a regular basis, with a reliable measuring device and end up with reliable results related to hat size, but the measurement would not be valid, because hat size is not related to the aspect that is being measured – that of intelligence.

An overview of tools for data collection

The key principle, then, in choosing methods for data collection, is to use the right tool for the job. Remember that a carpenter would not use cement to join wood together, just as a bricklayer would not usually choose screws and nails when building a wall! Alison sums this up very well:

> I see data collection as a means of documenting information in order to perform a study or analysis of something ... in effect we use these skills on a daily basis ... . For the purpose of action research, I will need to give careful consideration to the methods, to ensure the data collected are valid and usable in terms of interpretation and that I can make deductions from them. I see this task as harnessing the skills which I have and making the transition from informal chat and assumption, to recordable and measurable data that are both ethical and useful for the purpose.

You have probably already come across a range of data-collection tools in your reading around research methods. Within an action research project, you may use two or three different methods; for example, questionnaires, interviews, observation or focus groups. In addition, you may use video/DVD recording, audio recording and a range of note-taking techniques in order to capture successfully the information you have. Finally, other documentary evidence such as pupil records, work from children's books or school documentation may give important background information for your work or may prove to be valuable sources of data in themselves.

Alison started her project by producing a map of potential data-collection methods (Figure 3.1) and related issues. Many of these are discussed fully during the rest of the chapter, starting with the method that is usually most accessible for school-based practitioners: observation.

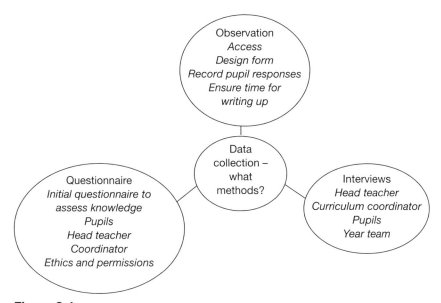

Figure 3.1

Observation

'Observation is not simply a question of looking at something and then noting down the facts. Observation is a complex combination of sensation (sight, sound, touch, smell and even taste) and perception' (Gray, 2004: 238).

Observation, therefore, is more than just looking! It involves systematic, close viewing of actions, the recording of these actions, and, most importantly, the analysis and interpretation of what has been seen. It is this last element that can cause difficulties. Any interpretation of a situation will be influenced by the person doing the interpreting and analysis. This may bring subjectivity and bias to the data collection. In other words, there is a danger that we will 'see' what we want to see and interpret what we see according to our own preferences, perceptions and previous experiences.

The observation spectrum

We saw in Chapter 1 that action research can be situated within the qualitative, interpretivist research paradigm. Similarly, data-collection tools often sit within a spectrum, ranging from the quantitative, or structured, to the qualitative, which may be more open-ended and interpretivist in nature, as exemplified in Figure 3.2.

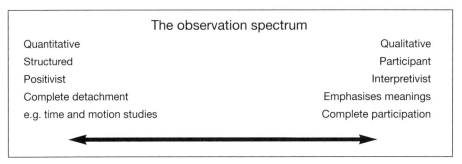

Figure 3.2

Structured observation

Structured schemes of observation often use predetermined categories against which observations may be checked. This can be done in various ways. For example, event sampling involves making a tally against a statement each time it is observed, whereas instantaneous sampling involves the observer entering an observation at standard time intervals. In addition, interval recording charts what has happened during the preceding interval, and rating scales seek to make a judgement about events being observed, as for example, by grading an event from one to five. While structured observation has many advantages, including high levels of reliability and ease of analysis, it must be remembered that for the data to be collected, the observer must be in the right place at the right time. In addition, structured observations usually capture only overt actions – it may be that further, unstructured observations need to be made in order to ensure that a full picture is built up of an activity.

Non-structured observation

A more qualitative, unstructured approach to observation does not exclude interesting but unexpected events. For example, a narrative description of classroom events may be focusing upon behaviour, but may actually highlight other areas of significance to the researcher. A structured, quantitative observation would not have that flexibility. In essence, a qualitative approach allows for the telling of a story – the story of classroom life, playground games, peer group relationships, or whatever it is you have chosen to study.

Whether you choose to use quantitative or qualitative methods, observations can be made from 'inside' or 'outside' a situation. In other words, you may take on the role of participant or non-participant observer.

Participant observation

Participant observation is aligned with ethnographic methodology, or the act of studying people in their natural settings or 'fields'. As a participant, the researcher becomes part of the group being researched, and understands the situation by experiencing it. In this respect, the observer tries to see life as it really is. However, in doing so, the observer inevitably influences what is going on around them to the extent that their gender, race, social background and a host of other factors will affect the research being undertaken.

Participant observation is common when conducting research within educational settings where practitioner research is being undertaken. There can be significant advantages to this approach, including, for example, ease of access, an understanding of organisational 'politics', and perhaps quicker and more successful identification of issues for investigation and their possible solution. However, the disadvantages should not be underestimated. For example, it could be difficult to adopt a fresh perspective if immersed in the organisation's ethos and attitudes, resulting in a research study that could be open to criticism of bias and subjectivity.

Non-participant observation

The non-participant observer will seek to operate in a more detached way than the participant observer. The observation may be more structured and may strive to be unbiased, but there are still dangers. Outsiders may be able to detach themselves emotionally from a situation, but may need to work harder to interpret events accurately and to ensure that all contextual issues are fully understood when the data are being analysed.

Using observation schedules

Observation schedules can aid observation and analysis. Although you will need to consider your key question of 'what information am I trying to capture?', the way observations are recorded is often a matter of personal preference. You may use graphs, charts, free flow text, diagrams, or a combination of different elements.

When deciding which strategy may work best for you and your particular research study, you may want to use the checklist in Figure 3.3.

Teaching assistants gathering data: Leanne's reflections on the use of observation

Nisbett (1977, cited in Bell, 1999) found that observational evidence gathering is not an easy option. He believed that it is a highly skilled methodology which requires extensive background knowledge and understanding together with the ability to spot significant events.

Through the use of non-participant observation, (that of watching the behaviour of the child from outside the situation), it was hoped that I would be able to record any actions that may occur during the activity. However, it was evident in the first week that I had not mastered the use of observational methodology. The non-participant observational schedule, devised using our school's generic observation form, included areas which resulted in the inclusion of repeated information. The observation schedule was therefore amended, resulting in the removal of the conclusion element.

Qualitative methods such as these reflected the purpose of the action-based research and the evidence collection that was hoped to be achieved. However, it was evident that the recording of significant events by both photographic and observational methods relied largely on my own interpretation.

Study focus	What is it that I want to find out?
Specific questions	Am I describing or understanding a situation? Am I trying to quantify the occurrence of certain events? Am I making comparisons?
Observational focus	Pupil behaviour? Pupil talk? Teacher activity? Social interaction?
Recording	Schedule? Will I invent one myself? Will I use pen/paper? ICT? Tape? Video?
Where?	Own class? Other class? Outside? Staff room? Will it be disruptive?
Problems	Observing may be intrusive – what problems do I anticipate?
Supplementary information	Will observational data alone be sufficient? What other evidence do I need?
Data processing	Are the data quantitative or qualitative? What processing and analysing techniques will be appropriate?

Figure 3.3 Observations checklist

TASK 3.1

HLTA 3.2.2   Monitor pupils' responses to learning tasks and modify approach accordingly.

Design a classroom observation evidence record form that could be used to collect research data. This could be used for observing an individual pupil, a group or the class. See Appendix 3.1 for an example.

Diaries, journals and field notes

Research diaries (also called journals or field notes) can be a useful record of observations, key points in the research process, significant events, or your feelings about the project and the direction it is taking. Any diary notes may be made on several levels:

- Raw data of observations made of people, the environment, their conversations, with dates, times, etc. These notes will be made 'in the field' as events are happening.
- Reflection and recall – expanded notes made after the event, when you can add other significant information that comes to mind.
- Themes and insights – a running record of analysis and interpretation.
- Experiential data – a log or journal of how you feel about the research process or significant events that have happened.

Any diary, journal or field notes must be as comprehensive as possible; often, such notes will enrich your project by adding important supplementary information. However, in producing field notes, you, as the researcher, will bring personal meaning to the account, possibly leading to an overly subjective account. It makes sense, therefore, that other forms of data collection are often used to support field notes.

Documentary sources

Bell (1999: 106) states that 'most educational projects will require the analysis of documentary evidence'. The most common kinds of evidence needed for a school-based action research project will be largely written as printed sources. For example, these could include pupil records, work from children's books or school documentation (such as minutes from meetings, policies, attendance registers, prospectuses, etc.). However, in addition, it may be appropriate for you to gather evidence of a non-written kind, such as pupils' drawings, models, or photographs related to display, or relevant project work. Such evidence may give important background information for your work or may prove to be valuable sources of data in themselves.

Questionnaires

Essentially, questionnaires contain a set of questions which people are asked to answer in a predetermined order. They are one of the most popular data-collection tools, and are often, mistakenly, thought to be easy to design and deliver. However, this is not always the case! Indeed, Bell (1999: 118) notes, 'It is harder to produce a really good questionnaire than might be imagined'. As with all data-collection tools, think carefully about exactly what information you are looking for before you design your questionnaire.

A questionnaire is only as good as the questions within it. Furthermore, a questionnaire that you design will reflect your views of the project, regardless of how objective you try to be. When writing individual questions, it needs to be remembered that people may interpret questions in different ways, so it is essential that questions are phrased as clearly as possible. There are also other general points to consider when writing questions, including the following:

- Are questions clear?
- Are questions concise? (Have you used 30 words, when 10 will do!)
- Do you avoid jargon and abbreviations?
- Does the wording of the question lead to a particular answer?
- Is the use of language appropriate to the respondents?
- Will the language used mean the same to all respondents regardless of culture, nationality, etc.?
- How much do the questions rely on memory recall?

Most importantly, avoid language that is prejudicial, or contains any form of stereotyping linked to gender, race or disability.

Types of questions

You are probably familiar with the use of 'open' and 'closed' questions as part of your role in the classroom. Open questions have no definite answer and may have quite an extensive, full response. They often begin with words like 'What', 'Where', 'Why' and 'How'. Open questions may provide very detailed data, but could be difficult to analyse. On the other hand, closed questions will have pre-determined answers, which are often 'Yes', 'No', 'True' or 'False'. The answers could also be restricted as, for example, with multiple-choice questionnaires. Although restricted in scope, the answers to closed questions are easier to analyse than the open questions described above. One compromise could be to design a questionnaire that is predominantly made up of closed questions, but with opportunities for the respondent to make further comments in a more open way, as appropriate.

There are other formats for structuring responses to questionnaires, including asking respondents to choose from a list, to select from a category or to rank things in order. As always, the format you use must be fit for the purpose it is designed to meet.

When all goes according to plan, there can be many advantages to using a questionnaire when gathering data. For example, you may be able to gather quite a lot of information within a short timescale, and the questionnaire format should make it relatively easy to analyse the information gathered and to present your results. However, all this does depend on a good response rate. If the response rate is too low, the validity of the information received may be compromised.

Interviews

Interviews have more flexibility than questionnaires. They give researchers the opportunity to follow up ideas and probe responses, thus potentially giving more detailed information than other forms of data collection. As with observation, an interview may be very structured or semi-structured. You may have set questions that you want to ask, or you may just have a list of prompts that you wish to explore. Whichever approach you choose, remember that the tool must be 'fit for the purpose' – always bear in mind what it is you are trying to find out. On a practical note, it is virtually impossible to write down everything that is said in an interview, so ensure that you tape-record and subsequently transcribe what is said by all those taking part. However, remember that transcribing tapes is a time-consuming business!

When conducting the interview, it is worth remembering a few basic points:

- In general, ensure that you have a quiet, comfortable room for the interview.
- Test all recording equipment beforehand and have spare batteries/power leads.
- Explain what the interview will be about and try to ensure that the interviewee is relaxed.
- Know what you want to ask – how structured will your questions be?
- To avoid bias, do not ask leading questions.

Interviewing pupils

It is likely that if you are working in a school, you will want to interview pupils for part of your project work. The same principles stated above apply with children, but it is often more challenging to phrase the questions in just the right way, in age-appropriate language. Most importantly, try to avoid leading children to say what they think you want them to say! With children, keep the focus very tight and keep the whole process short. In addition, ensure that the environment or circumstances of the interview do not affect their responses in any way. For example, a child who is missing playtime in order to be interviewed may not view the process very positively. Sometimes it may be appropriate to use stimulus material in order to start an interview or discussion. Such material could be a visual aid, such as a poster, book, toy or other object, or it could be a video clip or audio recording that relates directly to the child. Alternatively, children could have been involved in keeping diaries related to specific aspects of classroom life that may be a useful starting point for discussion. It should also be remembered that an individual interview might feel quite intimidating for a child. In this respect, being interviewed with a peer group may be less intimidating.

Group interviews

These can be a useful way of saving time in the busy school environment, whether you are interviewing adults or children. However, once a group is formed, answers may be influenced by the social nature of the exercise, and this must be considered in any analysis of data. On the positive side, group interviews can develop rich discussions, often generating a wider range of responses than an individual interview.

Teaching assistants gathering data: Alison's reflections on the use of questionnaire, observation and interview

> *The target for my research project is to use three forms of data collection, so there is a need to combine tools that I am comfortable with using, with tools that will collect the information I need. The use of a questionnaire will be the most relevant and essential tool for documenting the knowledge of my target group before, during and after the project. The form will contain very specific closed questions with right or wrong answers. I will also use observation of children in the vicinity of the display, to gauge their reaction. Gathering information about their comments will give scope for reflection. Whatever the outcome, I can ask 'why' questions: 'Why did they find that interesting?' 'Why does nobody bother to look at it?' This will ensure critical reflection. The third method will be interview. I am not too comfortable with formal interviews of staff members. To overcome this, I will keep the interviews short and to the point. If I choose only members of staff with whom I am comfortable I will not develop my skill, nor will there be a broad spectrum of opinions and views for my report.*

Using audio-visual equipment

Photography, and audio- and video recordings can be used to capture evidence when collecting data. Gray suggests that, within action research, 'photographs or video can be used to present evidence of changes' (Gray, 2004: 385). Audio recordings can be valuable in providing a detailed record of formal interviews or informal conversations with either individuals or groups. But, beware! Often a tape will need to be accurately transcribed before it can be analysed, and this takes time. For example, an experienced transcriber will usually allow around five hours of transcription time for an hour's worth of recorded material.

If you were considering using audio-visual equipment to support your data collection, it would be worth investigating what is available for use in your setting, just as Alison did.

Teaching assistants gathering data: Alison's investigation of audio-visual equipment

Within my setting, a large amount of audio-visual equipment is available.

Dictaphones would be beneficial for recording my own thoughts or comments when carrying out observations, giving me the opportunity to describe what I had seen and initial thoughts regarding its relevance. They are suitable only for very close, personal use due to sound quality.

Listening centres and portable tape recorders would be useful for recording interviews with staff members and children. Agreement would need to be sought in advance to protect confidentiality. The quality of recording is good, and, providing a suitable interview area was set up to avoid interruptions and background noise, quality evidence could be submitted and reflected upon. The disadvantage of this method is the possibility of intimidation by the process itself – in particular with children, whose quality of behaviour and responses may be affected.

Video and DVD recording is beneficial in recording evidence, but the ethics of the obvious identification of participants and inclusion within a report would have to be thoroughly researched. Permission would have to be obtained from parents, who might wish to see the recording in order to assess the contents.

Digital cameras could be used to photograph evidence, providing permission was sought from participants. Once again, parental permission would be needed, and the process of gathering permission could prove lengthy and time-consuming when weighted against the usefulness of the evidence.

Research ethics

Regardless of which data collection tools you use in your research, ethical guidelines must be followed. If you are studying for an academic qualification, your institution should have a set of ethical guidelines, usually posted on its website. Ensure that you are familiar with these, as well as the guidelines issued by the British Educational Research Association (BERA), which many institutions have adopted to support their research ethics policies. It is important to remember that, as an action researcher, your research is inextricably part of your existing educational setting. Therefore, it is worth noting that 'the failure to work within the general procedures of that organization may not only jeopardize the process of improvement but existing valuable work' (Hopkins, 2002: 195).

It is usual to give participants a project outline (explaining the purpose of the research) and to get written permission from anyone who will be taking part. This is called the principle of informed consent. If children are involved, parents will need to give consent. In addition, you may have in your workplace relevant policies that will need to be consulted, such as those on the use of video equipment or photography in school. It is important that participants are not named and that confidentiality is respected. Furthermore, you should always give participants the right to withdraw from the project at any time. In summary, you should:

- *Inform* your workplace of your research intentions.
- *Seek* permission from everyone who will be involved.
- *Consider* use of ethical guidelines for research; for example, British Educational Research Association (BERA): **www.bera.ac.uk/publications/pdfs/ ETHICA1.PDF**

Teaching assistants gathering data: Alison's reflections on ethical issues before the start of her project

I will submit my project proposal in full to the head teacher and to class teachers in order to ensure that any problems in relation to data collection methods or the feasibility of tasks will be identified early on. The written permission of these staff members will ensure that my evidence is useable. I will also need to ensure confidentiality regarding the identities of children and adults taking part in the project.

...and after the project

I was unable to gain the precise written permission from the head teacher, as I would have preferred, but her verbal agreement and support were given. In addition, one of the teachers left without returning the form. These issues served to highlight some of the ethical difficulties we face when gathering data.

Auditing your data collection skills

Before you finally decide which methods to use for data collection, use the checklist in Figure 3.4 to consider your experience and skills and any practical issues that may arise.

Getting organised

Finally, having read this chapter, you may be in a position to start to get more organised with your research project. In order to check your readiness, try task 3.2 overleaf.

Method	My experience and skills	Practical issues for my school? Resources? Appropriate for my setting?
Field notes/ journals/diaries		
Interviews		
Questionnaires		
Observation		
Tape recordings		
Video/DVD recordings		
Photography		

Figure 3.4

TASK 3.2

HLTA 1.6 Be able to improve own practice, including through observation, evaluation and discussion with colleagues.

Ask yourself the What? How? When? Where? Who? questions in Figure 3.5. If you are struggling to answer some of these fundamental questions, you may need to think more carefully about your research design. Try discussing it with fellow students or your mentor at school.

TASK 3.3

HLTA 2.9 Know a range of strategies to establish a purposeful learning environment.

Spend a few minutes reflecting on what knowledge and skills you have gained from reading this chapter. You could complete a mind map or spider diagram, noting down what you know, or you could use the checklist in (Figure 3.6) to assess your progress against the chapter objectives.

What?	What action?
	One curriculum area?
	Cross-curricular?
	A non-curriculum issue?
How?	What research strategy?
	What literature?
When?	Daily action?
	Weekly action?
	Same/different times?
Where?	Classroom?
	Outside?
	Quiet room for interviews?
Who?	Pupils?
	Adults? (classroom cover/taking part in research?)
Resources?	Questionnaires
	Schedules
	Prepared in advance?
	Use of ICT, tape-recording equipment, photography, video?
Recordings?	Notes – where, when, how much detail?
	Observations – how often? Detail? Non-verbal behaviour?
	Analysis of questionnaires and interviews? How?
Permissions?	Parents?
	Senior managers?
	School policies?
	Ethical guidelines?
Structure?	Is the study tightly structured?
	Will the action provide evidence to answer the question?

Figure 3.5

I know about some different methods for collecting research data
I could start to evaluate the appropriateness and effectiveness of different data-collection methods
I can consider the practicalities involved in collecting research data
I know the importance of considering ethical issues related to data collection

Figure 3.6

Key points

- Data can be collected by a variety of methods.
- Choice of 'tool' depends on the job in hand – consider what you want to show before deciding the data-collection method.
- Make sure you fully consider the wider ethical implications of your research and that you retain confidentiality.
- Keep key people informed of what you are doing.

Analysing the Data

Min Wilkie

This chapter will help you to:

- appreciate the importance/significance of the analysis of data
- consider some of the ways it is possible to draw conclusions from data and interpret findings
- consider how to display/record findings in order to facilitate interpretation
- become familiar with terminology and methodology
- evaluate the robustness of a project.

During any research project, you will have gathered data from a number of sources, and probably in a variety of ways. The challenge is to know how to use the data constructively. In order to do this, it will be necessary to impose some order on the material, to present it in a way that allows you and others to interpret what you found out. This process will require you to study data – this will involve looking for trends, incidences, patterns, themes (Macintyre, 2000: 91). As Brown and Dowling (1998: 80) point out, analysing data is 'the stage that causes the greatest anxiety and is the least likely stage to be made explicit'. I agree. In wanting to advise students, I have found that many books which discuss research seem to gloss over how to analyse findings. In Chapter 1, you were introduced to the interpretivist and positivist paradigms, which are normally aligned with qualitative and quantitative approaches respectively. A consideration of quantitative data would lead to a fairly complex study of statistical analysis. I do not propose to consider this in depth, as engaging in action research is regarded as qualitative, and projects in schools will normally involve small-scale projects that do not generate large numbers. Blaxter et al. (2001: 197) believe that it is rare to find data that are truly qualitative or quantitative; in fact they argue that each kind can be turned into the other. Brown and

Dowling (1988) advocate the 'dialogical use of a combination' of analyses, in other words, using data of both kinds to complement each other. I shall be investigating these views further below.

Freeman (1998: 96) describes the process of action research as investigating what, as a researcher, you feel you know already, but in carrying out investigation, you push yourself 'to examine the sense of certainty, to expose, to scrutinise, to question, not because you are mistaken but to find out what is true and why'. To do this, he believes disassembling and reassembling data is a vital process that is both engaging and challenging. He identifies four activities that are necessary to analysis:

- naming
- grouping
- finding relationships
- displaying.

I intend to consider these activities to explain how to make an effective analysis of small-scale research projects. All researchers need to consider significance, generalisability, reliability and validity (Blaxter et al., 2001: 221). I will also endeavour to explain these terms and discuss how far they apply to specific examples of action research.

Very often, students gather interesting and vibrant data through observations or surveys, but then they seem at a loss to know how to handle the information and make it work, by applying it to their objectives. Early in her work for the Foundation degree (FdA) in educational studies, Louise chose three children to observe (one each from the higher-, middle- and lower-ability numeracy groups from a Year 3 class of 27 mixed-ability pupils) in order to compare their strategies for addition and subtraction. She carefully recorded their responses and her initial interpretations, displaying them in a tabular format (Figures 4.1–4.3) that makes the information accessible, having introduced the task:

> *I explained to the children that I was going to ask them some adding and taking away questions. We discussed the fact that there are different ways to do the same sum and I told them it did not matter how they did it, but that I would like them to either write down their workings out or describe to me how they had found the answer.*

She then analysed her findings. Louise has perceptively assessed strategies in use, and told a 'story' that is useful in this small case study. In order to have done this, she was looking for incidences of strategies that she had 'named' as a result of learning about them. For instance:

- counting on
- using a derived fact
- partitioning and recombining.

Child A is in the highest ability group and showed a good range of strategies, although, perhaps, she did not always pick the most suitable. For example, when calculating 11+4, she used a strategy of approximating and adjusting, but it would have been easier to count on from the first number. Child A has taken on board strategies that are being taught in the class, and we can see that she is practising them and hopefully discovering for herself when best to use a range of different strategies.

Question	Answer	Child's explanation	Comments
11+4	15	11–1=10 10+4=14+1=15	Approximate and adjust
84+10	94	84–4=80+4=84 84+10=94	Got the correct answer but could not explain the beginning of the calculation. Said she had counted on in 10s in the second part
30+40	70	4+3=7 7+0=70	Using knowledge of place value
17+3	20	1+3=4 7+4=11	Her workings out are wrong but the answer is correct. I think she knew that 17 and 3 were a number bond making 20
48–45	3	40–40=0 8–5=3	Partition and recombine
60–30	30	'I just knew it'	Did this one mentally, using a known fact
15–5	10	10+5=15	Counting up – recognising that subtraction is the inverse of addition and using this fact to calculate the answer
50–25	25	50–20=30 30–5=25	Partitioning

Figure 4.1 Child A – higher ability

Child B has developed better strategies generally and seems to have a good understanding of mathematical concepts and strategies. He knows and uses his number bonds and recognises the link between addition and subtraction. He relied on counting on for most of the additions, but, perhaps, if the questions had involved larger numbers, he would have chosen and demonstrated different strategies.

Question	Answer	Child's explanation	Comments
11+4	15	'Put 11 in my head and counted on four'	Counting on from the first number in 1s
84+10	94	'Put 84 in my head and counted on 10'	Counting on from the first number in 1s
30+40	70	'Put 30 in my head and counted on in 10s'	Counting on from the first number in 10s
17+3	20	'I just knew it'	Using a known fact – number bonds to 20
48–45	2	'I counted back'	He got this one wrong. First counting back in 10s and then in 1s. A better strategy here would have been counting up.
60–30	30	'I just knew it' cos if you add 30 and 30 that makes 60'	Using a derived fact (6–3) to work out a new one or use of doubles
15–5	10	'I just knew that one as well' cos 10–5 is 15'	Using a known fact, a very quick response to this question
50–25	35	'I counted on in 5s'	Counting up – recognising the link between addition and subtraction

Figure 4.2 Child B – middle ability

Child C, who is of lower ability, still tries to calculate by counting on, using her fingers. This worked quite successfully with the additions, but she did not appear to understand the subtractions, with the exception of 15–5, which she did by counting on the 100 number square that is displayed on the classroom wall.

Question	Answer	Child's explanation	Comments
11+4	15	11 in head, counted on 4	Counted on from the first number in 1s – using fingers
84+10	94	84 in head, counted on 10	Counting on from the first number in 1s – using fingers
30+40	70	3+4=7 and then put a 0 on the end	Using knowledge of place value, or this may just be use of a taught procedure
17+3	20	Counted on	Counting on from the first number in 1s – using fingers
48–45	6	No explanation	She guessed this one after telling me that she could not do it
60–30	4	Guessed	She had no strategy to work this one out
15–5	10	Counted on	Counted on using the 100 square displayed in the class
50–25	6	Counted on	Tried counting on with her fingers

Figure 4.3 Child C – lower ability

These *codes* can come from 'outside', as in this example where strategies are already identified, or they might be determined from the data itself, as in another example.

Louise might have grouped together incidences from all three children, as in Figure 4.4, thereby enabling analysis of the most common strategies used by these children. In Year 3, where children are being taught to partition, only the most able child used this approach. Had Louise taken a greater *sample*, it would have been possible to see whether a relationship between the use of more sophisticated strategies and more able children was evident. This might have then affected the organisation of teaching.

Strategy	No. of incidences
Counting on/back	9
Using a known/derived fact	7
Partitioning and recombining	3
No strategy/guess	2

Figure 4.4

Louise used her data in a *qualitative* way, but there was potential also to manipulate the data *quantitatively*. The *validity* of her small study rests on her interpretation of the children's actions and their explanations agreeing. Having a video of the action would have allowed for a third check on the *internal consistency*, which is often referred to as *triangulation*. The *reliability* of her study depends on the ability to replicate and generalise the work. The conditions of the activity were made clear, so replication would be possible, but one would need a far larger sample to be able to assume that similar findings could be generated in any such situation. Generalising findings to other situations is not usually expected in action research, where small-scale research is frequently reported in a case study format and often does not present numerical data. It is important, however, in any study, however small, to explain in enough detail for the work to be *replicated* if another researcher wished to do so.

TASK 4.1

HLTA 3.2.3 Monitor pupils' participation and progress, providing feedback to teachers, and giving constructive support to pupils as they learn.

Chris carried out an observation, this time in a Year 6 history/geography lesson where the topic was Britain since the 1930s. Photocopy the observation and use different colours to highlight commonalities in behaviour displayed by child C and child D. Group these together and decide on some codes (up to four) that list behaviours. Place these in the parentheses at the side of the observation. Then count them up and enter them in the table in Figure 4.5. You may then be able to see at a glance which child is more likely to meet the lesson objectives.

Observation

I carried out an observation of two children during a session to assess what their understanding was and whether they were able to achieve the objectives for the lesson. The lesson was a follow-up of the previous session in which they had watched a video. Throughout the observation, references will be made to the two children, whom I shall refer to as C and D.

Introduction to lesson – seated in whole-class group on carpet

C	fidgeting/chatting/facing away from teacher.	( )
D	staring at display.	( )

Discussion considered changes to Europe since the First World War.

C and D	no involvement in group discussion, no interaction with teacher, as by eye contact/ non-verbal gestures.	( )

As session progressed

    D   shows some signs of participation and puts
                  hand up to answer question.   ( )

    C   answers question – 'How did Hitler feel?' –
                  inappropriate response.   ( )

                                                      ( )

*Teacher then explained what was required for the lesson – handing
out two sheets, a map and an instruction sheet. Teacher asked children to listen carefully. The second sheet told the children exactly
what they were going to do. Children asked to look at and read
through the sheet.*

    C and D   seem to be reading sheet.   ( )

*Group discussion took place on meaning of terms such as 'allies',
'neutral', etc.*

    C and D   appear to be interested in map.   ( )

*Teacher explained instructions, i.e. in what order, how and in what
colour.*

    C and D   appear to be listening and attempting to
                    read text.   ( )

    C and D chatting.   ( )

*Teacher then read the whole sheet to the whole class explaining what
was required.*

    D   not looking at map, instructions or the teacher. ( )

    C   able to contribute to discussion on reading
                  key appropriately.   ( )

*The teacher explained that this was also a test of their ability to
follow instructions appropriately. Children returned to their desks to
start work on completing sheet. At this time, I checked child's understanding of task.*

| C | shows good understanding of what was required. | ( ) |
| D | appears to have understanding – however also states that all cross-hatched should be red. | ( ) ( ) |

Children commenced activity.

D	sharpens pencil.	( )
C	picks up a red crayon, starts looking around the classroom.	( )
C and D	look around room – distracted.	( )
D	initially colours Germany correctly, and then continues to colour all hatched areas red; hand up for help from teacher.	( ) ( ) ( )
C	does not complete in order – teacher had explained that this would help with recall.	( )
D	needs reshowing what he should be copying.	( )
C and D	teacher reiterates how instructions need to be followed so that they would understand how events had unfolded.	( )
C and D	teacher moves away; both stop working and start a discussion.	( )
C	tries to support D.	( )
D	begins playing with pen.	( )
D	playing with pen.	( )
C and D	chatting.	( )
C	starts to work independently when told to finish work before going out for break.	( )
D	asks to leave room as has pen on face.	( )
D	on return, teacher asks to finish instructions for colouring map; responds that he had done it, but in fact has coloured the whole of the map red.	( )

| D | when asked to do so, not able to find instructions that requested using blue/green. | ( ) |

At the end of the exercise, I asked each child what they had under-stood from the session.

| C | able to explain why countries were coloured the way they were. | ( ) |
| D | unable to explain why countries were coloured in a particular way. | ( ) |

Code	Behaviours including	Child C	Child D

Figure 4.5

See Appendix 4.1 for a completed example of this exercise. There is more than one right way to do this!

Miles and Huberman (1994) suggest 13 ways to reduce data and begin to make meaning from analysis. These include

- clustering information
- counting frequencies of occurrence
- seeing plausibility – using informed intuition to reach a conclusion.

It is very likely, on completion of the above exercise, that all three of these ways to manage data will have been used! As Patton (in MacIntyre, 2000: 93) points out, analysis must enable the researcher to move beyond description. It is not enough to report. One should, even in small-scale research, be asking 'to what extent?', making comparisons and qualifying judgements. The examples above relate to observations, although analysis of responses to open questions in interviews and surveys can be treated in a similar fashion. If closed questions have been used, coding will have already been decided, and handling the data generated is simpler. It may still be desirable to look for trends and patterns, and to group and cluster information. Obviously, in order to do this, you have to interpret the data, and even though you try to do this with consistency and integrity, no researcher is entirely free of bias. It is necessary, therefore, to retain an awareness of the effect your choices may have, and explain why you make them.

TASK 4.2

HLTA 1.2 Build and maintain successful relationships with pupils, treat them consistently, with respect and consideration, and are concerned for their development as learners.

Yasmin included some photographs in her study about setting up a school council. Studies can be usefully supported in this way, though no one can avoid making judgements from such data. Study the photograph (Figure 4.6). How would you analyse the situation in the picture? See Appendix 4.2 for some inferences!

Figure 4.6

Displaying data

There are many ways to display data purposefully to aid interpretation. Offering a visual depiction of findings enables the reader to form an impression with more impact than the reading of results. When deciding how to display results, it is a good idea to interrogate your chosen method before determining to use it. Does it do what you want it to? Try getting someone else to 'read' your display and tell you what interpretations they can draw from it. Students may be impressed by the ease with which eye-catching charts and graphs can be compiled by a computer. They are sometimes tempted to include quantities of graphic material that do not enhance their work by aiding interpretation. Yasmin used block graphs to show the results of a questionnaire in a useful way (Figure 4.7).

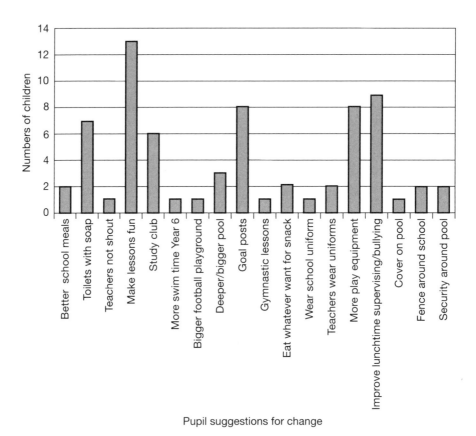

Pupil suggestions for change

Figure 4.7 Questionnaire responses regarding issues that pupils feel require change

Presenting data in this way has allowed immediate understanding that many children consulted had real and valid concerns, particularly about the way they are cared for. Some of these might have been grouped together – for instance, sporting suggestions might have been entered next to each other. Discussion and comparison opportunities open up in this way. Figures 4.8 and 4.9 examine the perception of the routes children felt were open to them to effect change in their school before and after a school council election and trial period. It is immediately evident that the children felt they had a viable new route after the project, although Yasmin might have made some changes that improved the impact. Retaining the same colours for categories, using the same scale for both graphs and ensuring consistency in labelling would all help. It would also have been possible to display both sets of information in one graph to facilitate comparison further.

In a study looking into the reading habits and preferences of a sample of Key Stage 2 children, Louise (not the same student as above) presented her data in both graphs and pie charts. In Figure 4.10, Louise can discuss the fact that the 'majority of pupils do, in fact, read a large number of books, outside school, for pleasure'.

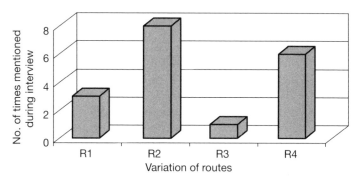

Key
R1 Teacher
R2 Head teacher
R3 Governors
R4 Outside agencies (council, police, government)

Figure 4.8 Routes suggested by children as a means for them to effect change

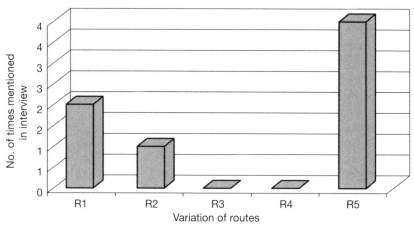

Key
R1 Teacher
R2 Head teacher
R3 Governors
R4 Outside agencies
R5 Suggestion box/school council

Figure 4.9 Final interview (post-council). Routes suggested by children as a means to effect change

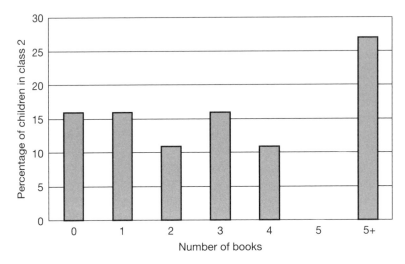

Figure 4.10 How many books do you read in a week?

However, she realised that her graph also shows that almost half the class read two books or fewer per week, and in following this up with the children, she confirmed that the books were quite often their own school reading books. Hopefully, they did enjoy these, but she was looking for additional, self-motivated reading, which was not discernible from the display she produced. From Figure 4.11, it is easy to see that the majority of children asked do enjoy reading, and this impression may be enough. Even when it is known that 18 children responded, it is not easy to work out exactly how many answered 'yes', although it is possible to speculate that one child does not like reading at all.

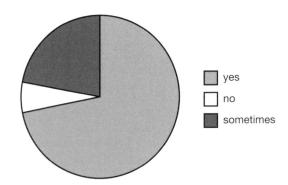

Figure 4.11 Do you enjoy reading?

Louise also showed in a similar way, that there is a spread in preferences for reading material (Figure 4.12).

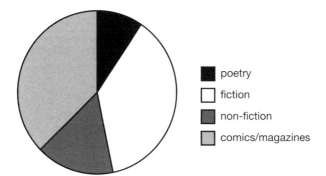

Figure 4.12 What do you like to read?

But it is not possible from these pie charts to see whether those children who like reading are the ones who like fiction and poetry, for example. In order to do this, one must correlate results. Sue (whom you met in Chapter 3) developed a study of the use of memory maps to aid the learning of children in Year 7. This involved training the children to make memory maps themselves, but Sue also endeavoured to compare the effectiveness of such techniques with alternative ways to present information. She did this by giving pupils the experience of working with information given in bullet-point form and given in memory map form. She then tested them for the retention of that information, and also asked them for their preferences. She then had data in the form of test scores and ratings for bullet points and mind maps respectively, which she was able to *correlate*, as shown in Figures 4.13 and 4.14.

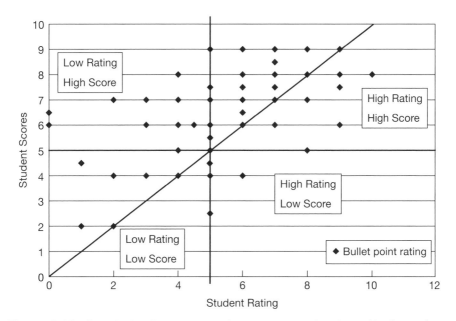

Figure 4.13 Correlation between student scores and rating of bullet points

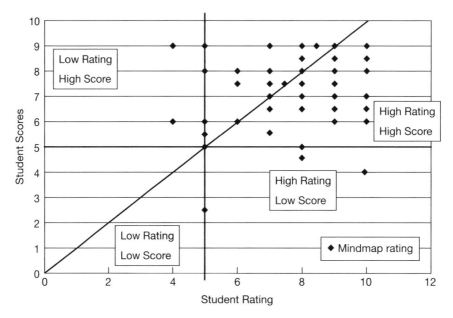

Figure 4.14 Correlation between student scores and rating of mind maps

---

TASK 4.3

HLTA 1.4 Work collaboratively with colleagues, and carry out roles effectively, knowing when to seek help and advice.

Working with a fellow student or colleague, make some statements by interpreting and comparing the graphs above. Are yours similar to those in Appendix 4.3?

In small-scale studies, one has to temper inferences with caution, as the numbers involved are usually too small to be significant, or to be generalised. I agree with Drever (1995: 70) that, in general, it is better to use actual numbers than percentages, for this reason. Often a simple table is a most effective way of displaying results. But, inevitably, although gathering information together and collating it as demonstrated above can help to make sense of data, there is also some 'degradation', some loss of quality. That is why balancing findings by reporting them using a variety of strategies will make the best of what you have. Jo, who works with dyslexic students in a centre apart from their school, examined the efficacy of various computer games in supporting learning (Figure 4.15).

Jo followed this examination with a discussion that began thus:

We can see that the Zoombinis games were the most often requested and favoured. The pupils played on the Zoombinis games for an average of 15 minutes; the other games were played for an average of 10 minutes. It

was noted in the observation sheets that the pupils remained more engaged with the Zoombinis games. They were often observed talking to themselves with a high degree of animation about the challenges and continued to play without pause until they were instructed to stop by the teacher.

It was also noted that when one pupil was playing Zoombinis, other pupils were drawn from what they were doing to watch and comment. This game produced more collaboration, peer interaction and conversation than any other. This was particularly evident when new Zoombinis games were introduced. The most confident and skilled players led the games and remained in control of the mouse. Other pupils gave help and advice where they were able; little conflict or argument occurred. Some pupils simply observed and waited until they had an opportunity to play the game more privately. The pupils were happy to ask for help from those who had demonstrated expertise. However, little help was sought from the staff other than to read the initial instructions.

Name of computer game	Number of times game requested during research period	Number of times voted favourite game in questionnaire
Zoombinis games x3	12	11
Numbershark	6	2
Wordshark	1	3
Catch-up	1	2
Starspell	0	0
Task Master	0	0

Figure 4.15 The number of times each game was requested and the game the pupils voted their favourite in the questionnaire.

In this example, Jo has given evidence numerically, by observation of their use, to justify that Zoombibis were the most requested games as well as by asking the children directly about their preferences; this double approach strengthens the reliability of her evidence. She has further enhanced this by giving qualitative analysis from observations about the students' behaviour, which would have been lost if she had presented only tables, and which is vital to assess overall success. I believe Jo's study exemplifies the way data from a small-scale piece of research can be analysed by both qualitative and quantitative methods that complement each other.

Key points

Strauss and Corbin 1998 (in Hopkins 2002: 130) advise classroom researchers of four important steps, which I have slightly rearranged to apply to this chapter in particular:

- Obtain valid and reliable data.
- Recognise, and where possible, avoid bias in interpreting and presenting data. Explain why you take the steps you do.
- Critically analyse the data – and choose methods to communicate what you believe is most important.
- Try to view what you have from the perspectives of others. Then you can approach an evaluation of whether you have communicated the essential information.

Writing the Report

Judith Baser

This chapter will help you to:

- plan the write-up of your study
- understand the purpose of a report
- understand the conventions for producing research reports in an acceptable format.

Planning for writing

At the start of your research project, think ahead – on completion, you will need to produce a report which will inform others about what you did, why and how you did it, how you assessed and evaluated it, what the outcomes were, and what recommendations you would make for the future. The temptation is to leave all this to the very end, and then rush frantically to complete it as the submission deadline draws closer. The best project in the world could be seriously undermined through being presented in a report that has been put together in a hurry, and is consequently poorly constructed and badly written.

Throughout the duration of the project, therefore, it is highly advisable to allocate time on a regular basis for writing up notes, evaluations, thoughts, ideas, reflection, etc., to provide a good, detailed learning journal, as discussed in Chapter 1. In this way, you can record the development and progress of the project, and will have plenty of material on which to call when writing it all up. Allow plenty of time for this when you plan your project, and be disciplined and firm with yourself about sticking to it; it is astonishing how quickly the days and weeks can fly by! Very few people have perfect memories, so it is not wise to rely on being able to remember everything – it is far better to keep written records, even if these are in simple note form.

You will, in fact, find it easier to produce a good final report by drafting parts of it as you proceed through the project. Near the beginning of the project, for example, you will have investigated other literature and research on the subject you have chosen (see Chapter 2). If this information is recorded and evaluated effectively at the time, you will already have formed the basis of your literature review section. As you make decisions about the methodology you will employ, that is, the means and methods for carrying out your research, you can begin to write this up, too. If you write up material as you go along in this way, you can gradually put together a draft outline report, which can be developed, extended, revised and ultimately refined into the final, polished product. This has the added benefit of ensuring that you have made a good start, in case life throws something awkward in your direction at just the wrong time, such as personal illness or family emergencies.

The computer can be both a blessing (when everything is working smoothly) and a curse (when it all starts to go wrong). When word processing, remember to save your work regularly and often, in several different places so that you have a back-up. It is perhaps also a good idea to print a hard copy from time to time, too, in case the electronic resources let you down. There is little more disheartening than the realisation that hours and hours spent on producing your masterpiece have been wasted because some technical problem (or, even worse, a stolen laptop) has made it inaccessible or wiped everything out.

Writing the report – a basic overview

The report is your means of explaining your research project and your findings to others. It needs to be clear, to communicate the content effectively, and the material should be organised into a coherent overall structure. To help you with this, reports of research generally follow a standard format. If you read plenty of academic journals, where research is often presented for the first time, you will notice that the content is organised into sections – you will find this useful to assist in the process of organising your material. The following information on report structure is fairly general, and is for guidance only. Seek advice from your tutor or supervisor, and consult any guidelines provided by your institution to ensure that you adhere to any necessary requirements regarding presentation and structure. Most reports will contain material that can be organised into appropriate sections in some form. The following can be used as a checklist for report writing:

- title-page
- acknowledgements
- contents list
- abstract/summary/synopsis
- introduction/context
- literature review
- methodology

- results
- analysis/evaluation/discussion
- conclusions
- recommendations
- bibliography
- appendices.

Each of these will be considered in more depth later in the chapter.

It is simply not possible to write a perfect first version of a report. You should consider the first or initial draft as exactly that – a rough version that will need considerable reworking, refining, reorganisation of content, etc., to produce a final definitive version. It is often a good idea to put together this initial draft, leave it for at least a day or so, and then return to it with fresh eyes. During the writing process, you may become too involved with the material; you know what is in your head, and what you want to say, but it is easy to read what you *think* you have written, rather than what you actually did write! Getting away from it all for a while helps you to return and review your work more objectively. Ideally, have someone else look at it too. This does not necessarily need to be someone who is familiar with the research material – it is a good proof of clarity and readability if a person with no connection to the content can read and understand it.

If appropriately knowledgeable, your helpful proofreader could also check for spelling and grammatical errors, and ensure that your meaning is clear. The advent of word processing has made it very simple to alter and rearrange words, sentences and whole paragraphs, and this can sometimes lead to errors creeping in unnoticed. Beware also of becoming too dependent on the spelling and grammar checkers provided – these do not always pick up words correctly spelt, but used in the wrong context (e.g., *there/they're/their*). Take particular care with sentence structure – the information in very long, involved sentences can often be conveyed more effectively in two or three slightly shorter ones (with the proviso that each sentence so formed is actually a grammatically complete sentence). This is where it can be so helpful to have someone else read through your work, to be what is often termed a 'critical friend' who can provide helpful comments on improving your work. However, choose your friend carefully – criticism should be appropriate, helpful and constructive, and not one of the 'forms of advice which can be very depressing and damaging to progress' (Cryer, 2000: 141).

Check how long your report is to be – a word allowance is usually given, and you should try to keep as close as possible to this. When you begin drafting the report, you might find it helpful to look at the sections you intend to include, and then allocate approximate numbers of words for each section. Keep purely descriptive material to a concise minimum. Try to find a good balance; you need to give the reader enough information to put the research into a context, and to understand what the project entailed, but not so much that you use your word allowance ineffectively. Markers tend to place more value on your analysis and evaluation of the material. You can help yourself with this by putting detailed factual or background information, which is relevant to under-standing the report, somewhere else – for example, this could be an appendix at the end of the report, or a portfolio of supporting material submitted with the report. Appendices or supporting material of this sort are not usually included in the word allowance.

Details of the required format for your report will normally be provided, giving information on such areas as width of margins, line spacing, font size, what is to be put on the title-page, overall length, etc. Make sure you read these and follow them exactly.

Writing style

Write in a straightforward, clear manner, using standard English, and avoiding informal language or colloquialisms (the type of phrase you might use in con-versation). Avoid the opposite extreme too – students (and, sadly, some academics too) sometimes seem to feel that academic writing requires the use of rather pedantic language, with long, convoluted sentences, packed with polysyllabic (long!) words. If your sentences are routinely spread over five, six or even more lines, you could probably split at least some of them into slightly shorter ones. Clarity and readability are important qualities; bear in mind that the people who mark work will have many reports to read, and do not want to waste time deciphering 'woolly' writing to extract the basic meaning. As Bell (1999: 208) points out, 'good, clear English remains good, clear English, what-ever the context. Technical language . . . rarely translates well onto paper and your readers (and your examiner) may become irritated by too much jargon or obscure language'.

You might like to note a small grammatical point to consider regarding sing-ular and plural words met in research:

One *appendix* (singular); two or more *appendices* (plural)
One *criterion* (singular); two or more *criteria* (plural)

Strictly speaking, both *media* and *data* are plurals, and should really be fol-lowed by a plural verb: 'different media are used', 'the data show that', although it is becoming more usual to find these used as singular nouns.

As far as possible, try to write with a reasonably intelligent, educated layper-son in mind as your target audience, rather than a particular expert in the subject area. Avoid making too many assumptions about what your reader might already know, and be prepared to clarify things that might not be obvi-ous. Most people can be expected to know and understand the more common standard terms used in education, but you may need to consider explaining subject-specific or technical jargon, particularly if it is not in common use, or is unusual or out of the ordinary. For example, most people have a reasonable idea of what the National Curriculum or the Literacy Hour are, but may not be so familiar with terms such as 'synthetic phonics' in connection with literacy, or 'decomposition' when talking about numeracy. This explanatory material has the dual effect of ensuring that your reader understands your meaning and providing evidence that you know and understand what you are talking about.

If you feel that your explanations are taking up too many precious words, perhaps you could provide an appendix with a glossary, a short dictionary listing the words and terms, and defining or explaining them.

Give abbreviations in full the first time you use them, with the short form you intend to use in parentheses after the term, as in 'special educational needs (SEN)'. You can then use the abbreviation throughout the work.

When writing reports of action-research projects, it is generally considered acceptable to use the 'first person' ('I did this, because …', 'it is my belief that…', 'my findings show that …'). First-person writing allows scope for plenty of personal reflection on your own role, and on any possible implications of the work, the findings, etc., for the development of your own practice and of practice within your setting. You are an integral part of the action-research process, so, as Bassey (1995: 68) advises, 'if you think you are in any way likely to be a variable in the conduct of the research and conceivably could affect the outcome, then write in the first person'. However, this is not always the case, as occasionally the passive voice ('it was found that …') is recommended to try to give an objective and neutral tone to your account, by eliminating the personal references. In the past, the use of the third person, that is, speaking of yourself as if you were someone else ('the current researcher felt that …') has been employed, although, as Bassey (1995: 68) rather scathingly comments, this does 'seem simply pretentious. It is an unworthy linguistic device to make the subjective masquerade as objective!' Consult your tutor or supervisor as to what is recommended, and always follow any guidelines provided by the institution.

Confidentiality

A key issue when reporting research that is about real people (particularly children) and real situations is confidentiality. Before embarking on the project work, check with the appropriate people in authority whether any official permission needs to be sought from parties who may be concerned in, or affected by, your work. This is particularly important when working with children, as it is sometimes necessary to obtain parental permission. Be guided by the rules and regulations of your setting, and keep strictly to them. Identities must be protected, and the reader should not be able to identify any participants in the research – use first names or initials only, give a different first name, or use something like 'child A', or 'Mr B' or 'teacher B'. Keep a thick, black, felt-tip pen and/or a bottle of white correction fluid handy to cover identifying names on any documentation you use to illustrate points or provide evidence. Photographic, video or any other electronic evidence also needs to be assessed with care, and any necessary permission sought, before it is used.

Referencing

Within your report, you will be expected to refer to the writing and works of others, for a variety of reasons: to illustrate, support and inform your points; to consider differing opinions and points of view; to offer critical appraisal; or even simply to demonstrate the thoroughness and range of your background reading and research! Whatever the reason, the key point here is that you identify the source of any reference as clearly and unequivocally as possible, to avoid any suspicion of plagiarism. Plagiarism, the presentation of the work of others as your own, is essentially a form of fraud or theft, and is considered to be one of the most heinous offences in the academic world. Being caught trying to pass off the work of someone else as your own can have serious repercussions, as work can be failed, and students caught have often been ejected from courses and institutions. It is therefore absolutely vital to acknowledge clearly where you have found your information. In brief, the main points are as follows.

Short direct quotations, marked by inverted commas, can be included within a paragraph, with the source's surname, year of publication and page number given in parentheses: 'Playing back tapes or making transcripts can be very time-consuming and expensive' (Hopkins, 2002: 105). Where possible, try to integrate quotations smoothly into your writing: 'Hopkins (2002: 105) makes the point that "playing back tapes or making transcripts can be very time-consuming and expensive", which I have found to be very true.'

Longer quotations should be produced as a small section of text that is separated out from the main paragraph and indented. See an example of this on page 71 in a quotation from Kember. Again, the author's surname, year of publication and page number should be given. Avoid very long quotations – tutors generally prefer to read your own ideas and words, rather than those simply taken from textbooks. You may sometimes need to summarise the key points of larger sections of text or ideas, in your own words. This is acceptable as long as you still explicitly acknowledge the source by adding the author's name and year in parentheses.

For Internet sources, it is not always so simple to identify the actual author, and material can be altered or disappear without warning. However, providing the Web page address and the date you accessed it should be sufficient.

Full details of the sources can then be provided in the bibliography (see page 73). Most institutions will provide helpful information and guidelines for referring to the work of others; find these, read them carefully, and follow them closely.

The report sections

Title-page

This is the first thing the reader will see, so you need to ensure that key information is provided clearly and legibly. This might include your name, any required reference information (such as student number, institution reference number, module/unit number, title or description of the research project, etc.), and any other details which may be needed. Again, be guided by the requirements of your own institution.

Acknowledgements

This section is not usually specifically required, but does provide you with an opportunity to mention key people who have helped you complete the project, and to offer your thanks and appreciation to them.

Contents list

This will be one of the last things to be written, once the main sections of the report have been put together, and you have a better idea of the content, organisation of material, sections, page numbers, etc. It should give the reader a good overview of the structure, organisation and content of the report, and should enable particular sections to be found quickly and easily.

Abstract/summary/synopsis

This is essentially a succinct summary of the contents of the report, limited to 200–300 words or fewer. When reading journals, you will usually find something of the sort at the beginning of each article or contribution, and it is there to give readers an overview of the content – it saves time and effort, as there is no need to read all the way through each article. 'Both the abstract and the paper should make sense without the other' (Bassey, 1995: 71). Your abstract or summary should therefore be as brief and concise as possible, but still communicate the main points of the report. Keep the focus clearly on the key points, eliminating unnecessary detail. It is not always easy to condense a report of several thousand words to just a couple of hundred, so it might be helpful to concentrate on providing answers to these questions:

- What was the rationale for the project, that is, its original starting point; why was the project carried out?
- What were the main aims and objectives of the research discussed in the report?
- What methodologies were used?
- Where there any ethical considerations to take into account?
- What were the outcomes?
- What conclusions were drawn?

Because you are writing about the report, which is still in existence here in front of the reader, rather than the research itself, which may well be finished and therefore in the past, the abstract may be written in the present tense (e.g. 'This report aims to …', 'the evidence demonstrates that …', or 'the findings show that …'). See Chris's abstract below for an example of this. However, a glance at abstracts in journals will often show the past tense being used. Check with your institution's own guidelines, and be directed by these.

Teaching assistants (TAs) writing the report

Chris, a TA supporting children with Special Educational Needs (SEN) in a secondary school, carried out an action research project which considered the effectiveness of a programme to help children cope with the transfer from primary to secondary school. In fewer than 250 words, Chris provided a good overview of the content of her 5000-word report. The reader can see at a glance what is in the main body of the text; it is clear why she did the work, how she carried it out and assessed it, what her findings were, and what recommendations she makes as a result of the research.

TASK 5.1

HLTA 1.6 Be able to improve own practice, including through observation, evaluation and discussion with colleagues.

Try some of the following strategies in practising writing abstracts:

1. Two ideas recommended by Blaxter et al. (2001: 261) are as follows:

   - Read a relevant book or article and try to summarise the 'subject ... its context, methodology and conclusions', taking 'no more than half an hour'.

   - Find a piece of writing which already has an abstract, and try writing one yourself without looking at the original. Then compare yours to the original.

2. Find a willing partner, such as a fellow student. Each of you chooses an appropriate piece of writing, such as a journal article or book chapter, and summarises its main points. Swap articles and summarise again. Compare your summaries. Are they similar? Have you both selected the same key points? If there are differences, examine these, and discuss why you each made the choices you did. Together, try producing a single summary.

Chris's project report abstract

> *As a result of the government's inclusion policy (DfEE, 1998c, in Cowne, 2000: 87), more vulnerable and special educational needs (SEN) students are now entering mainstream education than previously. In order for students to progress academically after they enter secondary education, they need to have a positive approach and to feel confident and comfortable in their new setting (Cowne, 2000: 64). This project aims to determine whether a transition programme introduced in the Spring term of Year 6 might have a significant and measurable impact on the progress and attitude of SEN and vulnerable students to their secondary education. Data are gathered through questionnaires to students and teachers, observations and interviews. A draft transition programme of six sessions is trialled, evaluated and reviewed with a group of ten Year 6 students. The sessions (some in the primary school setting, others in the secondary setting) aim to cover the main areas of concern during the transition period. The main findings are that a*

transition programme can help vulnerable and SEN students to adjust well and settle into their new school, with the result that they are likely to become better motivated throughout their subsequent schooling. Recommendations are made regarding activities that should be incorporated in the transition programme to ensure that it covers the most common and significant issues that concern primary school students at this time.

Introduction – basic contextual detail, rationale, aims of project

Remember that the person who will read or mark your work will not necessarily be someone who knows you, so, in your introduction, you should provide basic information about the circumstances of the project to give the reader a context. The reader needs some helpful background information to be able to understand the research more clearly. Is the project work set in a nursery, primary, secondary or special school? Is it based in the Foundation Stage or Key Stages 1, 2, 3 or 4? In a large, inner-city, multi-ethnic secondary school with 2000 pupils, or a tiny, rural primary school with under 100 pupils? Who are you and what is your role? Give the basic facts here, keeping the information concise and succinct. More extensive detail can be put into an appendix, supporting portfolio or learning journal.

Chapter 1 explained that action research needs to be 'practical and problem-solving in nature'. In this introductory section, then, it is sensible to identify the problem, challenge or issue, and explain how your proposed 'action' will address it.

Literature review

In Chapter 2, we looked at the importance of reading and research to support, illustrate and inform your project work, and how to evaluate it. In this section of your report, then, you need to summarise the key findings from your investigative reading. Try to give a good critical overview of the key texts and sources you have examined (although keep this as concise as possible – it should not become the main section of the report) that had relevance to your project work. Which sources did you find particularly useful, informative, encouraging or inspiring? Which were not so helpful, or perhaps contradicted or conflicted with others' views? Explain and expand upon your comments; it is not enough to simply state, 'I found Smith et al. very useful' (Haywood and Wragg's 'furniture sale catalogue', 1978: 2); you need to give valid reasons for your views. Keeping reasonably detailed records as you do your reading will ensure that you have a good foundation on which to build this section. Refer back to Karen's work in Chapter 2, and note how she has evaluated the sources she has considered. She has shown that she has consulted a good range of sources, and has selected those that she thinks were most relevant to the project work. You could also use the final paragraph of your review to show how your reading has helped you to formulate and refine your research question.

Methodology

In this section, your main aim should be to explain how you carried out your project: what you did, how you did it and why you chose the particular methods and assessment strategies employed. Initially, it may be helpful to restate the problem briefly, showing how it has arisen, and what the current effects are. With this as a context, you can then explain in more detail what 'action' you intended to apply to solve it, how you hoped this would work, and what the outcomes would be, thus identifying your main aims and objectives. This might be a good point at which to insert some suitable references to the action-research process itself, to demonstrate your understanding of the principles of this investigative paradigm, and their practical application.

Your next step is to describe the methods and means you employed to assess the project work and its outcomes. There should be some kind of initial, or baseline, assessment of the situation, with something similar at the end of the research period, for comparative purposes. When explaining your data-gathering methods, as well as describing them, you should include a rationale for your choices. Why did you choose to issue questionnaires, carry out observations, hold interviews, or use school test results? What did you hope to gain by carrying these out or using them? What was it about the participants, the setting, the situation, etc., that made you select one strategy rather than another? How, and why, did you select a particular group of children to work with, or your target group for questionnaires? As discussed in Chapter 3, it is helpful to be clear in your own mind about your reasons for gathering any particular information, to ensure its relevance to assessing the outcome of the work. Samples of questionnaires, observation sheets, interview questions, etc., can be placed in an appendix or supporting portfolio, so that the reader can examine them there.

You also need to explain what you intend to do with all this data. How will the information you collect be analysed? What will your results show, and how will they do this? This explanatory information will help to demonstrate your understanding of the research process. You are providing evidence to show that you clearly understand why you are collecting this information, what you think it will show, and how it will illuminate your project work, showing the effectiveness of the applied 'solution' to the identified problem.

Results

This section, although important, does not need to be too long. You simply need to state what your findings were. The temptation is sometimes to start analysing and evaluating the outcomes as you present them, but resist this, leaving this discussion for the next section. The presentation of this information is important, as it is at the heart of your research project, and your reader needs to understand clearly what the outcomes of the work were. What you include will of course depend very much on what you did and the nature of the data you collected, and may consist of a mixture of text, in which you describe the end results, and graphical information, such as tables, graphs and charts etc. Where you put all this information is a matter of choice. You can include it here, within this section of the report, or you can put it in a clearly–identified appendix, and refer the reader to it there. Make sure that any tables and graphs are clear, well labelled and comprehensible, and that their content and meaning is explained. It is also important to check that they are relevant, and really do support, inform or illuminate your presentation of the results. The reader is looking for evidence that you can provide pertinent information clearly and effectively, rather than simple proof that you have mastered the art of producing spectacular graphs on your PC.

Essentially, you are aiming to show how things were at the beginning of the project in contrast to how things stood at the end.

Analysis/evaluation/discussion

So, having identified the issue, thought up a possible solution, carried it out, achieved some results and considered them, what have you found out? Given the initial aims and objectives you set out with, has the project been an outstanding success, a dismal failure or something between these two extremes, a neutral zone with no evidence of either improvement or worsening of the situation? It is important to remember that the actual outcome of action research is not the key issue. In considering the 'process as outcome' Kember (2000: 217) says,

> The experiences of many participants suggest that in many ways the journey was more important than reaching the destination. In fact, it was often those who had to struggle most on the journey because projects did not turn out as anticipated who drew the greatest benefits.

Whatever the results, the point is to analyse and evaluate them, and use them as the basis for taking the work forward. This, then, is the section in which you examine the results presented in the previous one. Was the chosen 'action' successful in addressing the issue originally identified? What do the results tell you? Did they confirm your initial thoughts, showing that your idea was a sound one? Why do you think it all went so well?

If things unfortunately went awry, take heart. McNiff and Whitehead (2002: 90) offer the following comforting view:

> Learning from processes where things do not go right is as valuable as when they do. The struggle to make sense is the research process. It does not matter that an external situation does not go as one hopes. What is important is to be aware of the problematics, to use these as rich opportunities for learning, and to explain the process so that others can learn from the account.

What were the possible causes of the lack of success in achieving your aims? On reflection, if your suggested solution turned out to be ineffective in some way, what might be the reasons for the lack of success? Was it perhaps an intrinsic matter arising out of the nature of the 'action' chosen? Your idea may not have provided the hoped-for solution, or may have produced unforeseen and unexpected results, so you need to examine what happened and consider why it all turned out the way it did. Was the outcome perhaps affected by external influences in some way? Inevitably, there will be variables to consider – schools can often be very unpredictable places, and it is not always easy or straightforward to carry out a coherent, sustained piece of research over a reasonable length of time without meeting some problems. A whole host of possible causes of hitches can arise, such as changes to timetables (often a particular problem in the pre-Christmas period, or summer term) or to the TA role, staffing changes, reorganisation, management decisions, and children leaving (or even being excluded) or moving to different groups. All or any of these may have had an effect. Consider the action itself – could you have made different, or better, choices in what you decided to do? Did you have to make a lot of adjustments as you proceeded with the project? Were the data-gathering methods appropriate, giving you sufficient useful information? Students often find that they have collected a lot of information, much of which then turns out to be unhelpful, or difficult to use in a meaningful way.

Reflect on everything that has happened, and show how you understand the results, and any implications these may have for the situation, and for yourself, your role and your practice.

Conclusions/recommendations

You need to bring your report to a satisfactory end, by providing a final section in which you present a summary of your main findings, looking back at your original objectives, and explaining what conclusions you are drawing from the work you have done. Avoid introducing any new material or ideas at this final stage that should really have been presented in an earlier section; this final part is about summing up all that has happened, and finding meaning in it. This section could also present an opportunity for linking your own work to that discussed in your review of the literature, helping to fit your project into a context identified earlier. Having considered these, you can then provide some pertinent recommendations. Here, you can offer suggestions, on the basis of the results of your research, either for improving practice, by taking on board activities, strategies, etc. that were tried as part of the project, or for making any necessary alterations to the 'action' that would take the research forward onto the next cycle.

Bibliography/list of references

You must provide a full, detailed list of all the sources of material you have referred to throughout your report. The exact nature of this will depend on the institution, so ensure that you familiarise yourself well with any guidelines provided outlining the preferred method, which in academic institutions is usually the Harvard system, outlined below, listing works alphabetically by author. What you must include is sufficient information on each source to enable your readers to locate it and read it for themselves. This information can typically be found on a page at the front of the book, although, occasionally, some elements may be missing, unclear or difficult to locate. If this is the case for a book from the library, try looking it up in the library catalogue, or even the back catalogue often provided on the publisher's website, where you should be able to find the necessary details.

Books

Sources are usually listed alphabetically by authors' surnames. For each type of source, provide information as indicated as in Figure 5.1.

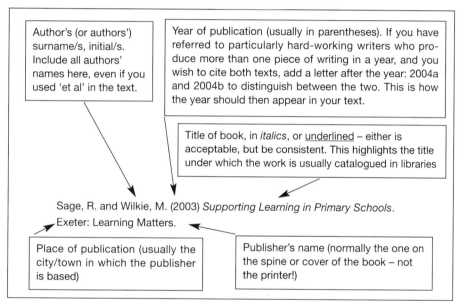

Figure 5.1

Journal articles

As well as the author name/s and year, give the title of the article in the same font style in inverted commas, and then the name of the journal (in italics or underlined, whichever style you have chosen), the volume number, the particular issue name or number, and the first and last pages of the article. For journal articles, the place of publication and publisher can be omitted. For example:

Mumtaz, S. and Humphreys, G.W. (2001) 'The effects of bilingualism on learning to read English: evidence from the contrast between Urdu-English bilingual and English monolingual children', *Journal of Research in Reading*, 24 (2): 113–34.

TASK 5.2

HLTA 1.4 Work collaboratively with colleagues, knowing when to seek help and advice.

Identify the missing information! Look at the following sample bibliography, taken from Sage and Wilkie (2003: 100), which has been severely tampered with! What information is missing from each item? What is wrong with the overall list? Check the correct version in Appendix 5.1.

Bandura, A (1973) *Aggression, a Social Learning Analysis*. Englewood Cliffs, NJ: Prentice Hall.

Ainsworth 'The development of infant-mother attachment' in BM Caldwell and HN Ricciuti (eds), *Review of Child Development Research* Vol 3. University of Chicago Press.

Bee, H (2000) *The Developing Child* (9th Edn). London

Bell, SM (1970) 'The development of the concept of object as related to infant-mother attachment', *Child Development*, 41: 291-31

Bell, N (1991) *Visualizing and Verbalizing*. Paso Robles, CA: Academy of Reading Publications.

Cooper J, Moodley M and Reynell J *Helping Language Development*. London: EA Arnold.

Dale (1976) *Language Development: Structure and Function* (2nd ed). New York: Holt, Rinehart & Winston.

Binet, A and Simon, T (1916) The Development of Intelligence in Children. Williams & Wilkins.

Borke, H (1975) 'Piaget's mountains revisited: changes in the egocentric land-scape', *Developmental Psychology*, 240-3.

Diorio, D, Viau, V and Meaney, MJ (1993) 'The role of the medial prefrontal Cortex in the regulation of hypothalamic-pituitary-adrenal responses to stress', *Journal of Neuroscience*.

Bowlby, J, Attachment and loss (Vol 1) *Attachment*. New York: Basic Books.

Brazelton, TB, Robey, JS and Collier, GA (1969) 'Infant development in the Zinacanteco Indians of southern Mexico' *Pediatrics*, 44.

Bruner, JS, Olver, RR and Greenfield, PM (1966) (eds) *Studies in Cognitive Growth*. New York: Wiley.

Cortes JB and Gatti FM (1965) 'Physique and self description of temperament', *Journal*, 20:432-9.

In this instance, 24 is the volume number, and (2) is the issue number.

For websites, give the name of the author and date posted on the Web (if known), and then the *full* uniform resource locator (URL), the unique address which identifies a resource on the Internet, not just the website, along with the date you accessed it:

Smith, M.K. (2001) **www.infed.org/research/b-actres.htm** (date accessed 19 August 2005).

Appendix/appendices

An appendix at the end of the report is the place to put extra material which gives extended, more detailed information, or provides relevant illustrative examples or documentation. Appendix material is not usually included in the word-count of the report; thus it is a sensible idea to put descriptive background and contextual information here, so that you can refer the reader to it in the relevant report sections.

Reviewing your work

As mentioned earlier in this chapter, after working through several drafts, and finally achieving what you think is a reasonable final version, it is helpful to put some distance between yourself and your work – leave it for a while, a couple of days rather than hours, and then return to it and reread it freshly as a whole. Does the report 'read' well? A good test of this is to try to read it out loud, although, as Bell (1999: 209) sensibly advises, 'make sure you are alone or your family may feel the strain has been too much for you!' Check that the content and meaning flow through the sections logically and coherently, with each paragraph following on from the last sensibly. Is the material in each section or chapter appropriate? Be honest with yourself – does your report give a good, clear, comprehensible account and analysis of the development and progress of your research project? Be brave and ask someone else to read it and give their opinions and views. You know what you mean and what you want to say, but until someone else reads what you have written, you cannot be certain that you have communicated your message clearly.

Hopkins (2002: 140) offers several sound reasons for taking care to write up your project thoroughly, believing

> 'that all teacher-researchers need to put their data together in such a way that:
>
> • The research could be replicated on another occasion.
>
> • The evidence used to generate hypotheses and consequent action is clearly documented.
>
> • Action taken as a result of the research is monitored.
>
> • The reader finds the research accessible and that it resonates with his or her own experience.

Once you have completed your report, you could perhaps consider it in the light of these points. Could someone else carry out a similar project with the information given in your report? Have you clearly identified your original aims and objectives, and explained how you worked toward achieving these? Have you applied appropriate actions during the research and observed their effectiveness? Is your account of the work effective in communicating exactly what happened, so that the reader can picture it clearly and relate to it? Be honest with yourself!

All that remains is for you to hand in your work by the deadline, and you can then go and reclaim your life!

Key points

- Be disciplined, and save, save, save!
- Write up notes as you go along.
- Adhere to any advised format carefully, and keep working on appropriate academic style.
- Leave enough time for review by yourself and others if possible to ensure clarity.

Benefiting from Action Research

Min Wilkie

This chapter will help you explore:

- how to prepare to 'defend' your report during a viva or share it through a presentation
- how action research projects can be used to influence continuing change and development
- how research and higher education study can contribute to the professional development of support staff
- some considerations in working as a member of a team while researching
- some considerations for working with other professionals.

The report is finished – what a sense of achievement! In carrying out the work that you have done, you are bound to have made some impact on those around you. Hopefully, you will want to share these ideas, especially with those who have a stake in your work – and not forgetting the children, who may be very interested in your findings if they are presented in an accessible way.

In the academic world, you are likely to share your work formally as part of the assessment procedure. This might be through a *presentation*, perhaps to peers, or by talking to people on a formal basis about your report, and answering questions. This is known as a *viva*, and the processes involved will be described further below. In the world of work, you are sure to want to continue to make educational experiences more worthwhile; otherwise, you might ask why do all that work? This chapter will also discuss some of the possible ways forward and attempt to point up significant considerations.

The viva

This is an oral assessment. Normally, there is time to consider your response in some way before it takes place. The model we use at the University of Leicester and Bishop Grosseteste College, Lincoln works as follows. Students bring a copy of their report with them to their appointment, and they can refer to this, or refer listeners to parts of it at any time during the interview. They know they will need to describe their report briefly as an opener to the process. This can be thought of as a verbal abstract. The listeners want to know something about

- the context in which you carried out the project
- your role
- what your focus was
- why you chose it
- how you carried out your research
- what happened.
- what you recommend as a result of your work.

TASK 6.1

HLTA 1.6 Be able to improve own practice, including through observation, evaluation and discussion with colleagues.

Find a willing listener and give them the questions listed in the section on writing an abstract in Chapter 5. Then try to explain your research project to them within a set time limit. Start with two or three minutes. Later you could try limiting yourself to perhaps one minute or even less! At the end of your summary, does your helper know the answers to the questions?

In our model, there are two listeners, and the viva is videoed so that moderation can take place later. On arrival, students are given a short time to consider two questions. They are permitted to make brief notes that they can bring into the interview with them. Bullet points, mind maps or flow diagrams are all suitable ways to do this. The object is to be able to speak from these without reading verbatim. These questions are generic, in our case, as it is important to give each student the same experience. They follow on from the opening description. Of course, the way the student answers will influence the ensuing conversation. Using evidence from the report, perhaps referring listeners to tables of results or particular findings, can be a helpful strategy. Remembering some key supporting research that you can include in your answers is also a good idea. The questions you have prepared are often followed by a final question that you will not have seen during preparation and that you will need to respond to spontaneously.

> **TASK 6.2**
>
> *HLTA 1.6 Be able to improve own practice, including through observation, evaluation and discussion with colleagues.*
>
> Preferably with a partner, make up some questions – at least one on each main section of your report. Then try to answer these within a given time limit. Refer to your report where you can.

The presentation

If this is the mode of assessment used, it is likely you will need to prepare a PowerPoint presentation that you can speak from. Using key words and phrases avoids slides that contain too many words. There are many techniques available to generate interest when creating slides. Try to be selective, and not to overpower your audience with fussy, distracting insertions. If you use notes, it is a good idea to have key words and phrases written clearly on cards that you can place on a table or surface. Following small type on an A4 sheet is difficult and will not allow eye contact with the audience. Number these and/or fix them together, as dropping them can have disastrous consequences.

Remember to introduce yourself, even if your audience has known you for some time, and follow this with brief details about the organisation of your talk. This 'verbal signposting' is useful in setting expectations for your listeners. Make sure there is a balance between describing how you set up your research and what you found out. You should include some recommendations, and summarise by restating your main points. Some of the exercises with peers in the section on vivas, above, will also be useful in preparing for your presentation.

Influencing continuing change and development

I have found that early in research, students often feel their reports must show success, and they concentrate on anything positive, ignoring the processes they have worked through and the occasions when they have changed their minds or made significant decisions along the way. Kember (2000: 217) stresses the importance of the journey; it is as important, if not more important, than the destination. He points out that those who struggle most because their projects do not develop as anticipated draw the greatest benefits. 'Unanticipated differences can and do lead to major reconsideration of deep-seated convictions about teaching practices.' This is worth remembering, as even small-scale studies in schools can enable TAs to learn, to make improvements in the way they work with children, to gain sufficient insight to pass on useful information, and maybe to repeat work involving more people (Kember, 2000: 212).

In Chapter 1, the idea of action research being cyclical in nature was introduced. SPEAR, a more recent model proposed by Warwick (2005), suggests a framework where some 'toing and froing' is quite in order … ideas are revised with a cycle of action. I recently spoke to some newly qualified teachers about working with TAs and other adults in the classroom. Part of this talk addressed the ways relationships can affect success in the classroom. A small group of the audience felt that, as new, lowly staff, they did not have the power to change policy and practice. I was disappointed with this negative attitude. Many of the TAs I have worked with, who are often employed on hourly rather than permanent contracts have been able to influence developments significantly. Change does not happen immediately, but asking the right questions in the right way, trying out and monitoring ideas, and so on, can be motivating for everyone concerned. Everyone involved with working with children should feel they *can* make a difference.

The professional development of support staff

Many now recognise that the TA role is a professional one (Farrell et al., 1999; Sage and Wilkie, 2003; Watkinson, 2002). This is corroborated by the introduction of higher level teaching assistant (HLTA) status in 2004, and in moves involved with the workforce remodelling that is taking place at the time of writing. Many TAs are now accorded significant professional responsibility; for instance, in covering for teachers' 'planning and preparation' (PPA) time, or in administering intervention programmes. TAs are no longer merely working under instruction. Since 1975, when Stenhouse began the promotion of teachers as researchers, the idea of actively evaluating practice in education has been accepted. Elliott (1991: 128) endorses the beliefs of Klemp (1977) regarding those who benefit most from action research: people whose occupations involve problem solving and decision making. The role of the TA certainly embraces these features! In fact, he lists the following cognitive and interpersonal abilities that will be developed. I would suggest that all of these are crucial to professional growth and successful teamwork:

- being able to discern thematic consistencies
- understanding controversial issues
- learning from reflection on experience
- well-placed empathy
- the ability to promote feelings of efficacy in others.

He suggests that engaging in action research involves taking 'cognitive initiative, being a performer, not just an actor, capable of changing situations rather than having things happen to you'. Macintyre (2000: xii) dubs those researching in schools 'active change agents', and points out that, by engaging in action research, students and professionals in school 'learn how to reflect and self-evaluate and so gain confidence in discussion and improving their teaching', leading to their being able to say not 'I think' but 'I know, because....', and making adjustments to better situations. During research, assumptions are examined and practice is changed in a controlled, deliberate way. Macintyre believes that, otherwise, change is intuitive and cannot be so readily justified. The action plan becomes part of general forward planning, and not a disruptive 'add-on'. Being able to justify one's intentions, having taken into account current educational developments, the needs of the children and documented work, increases the professional profile. Many of our foundation degree students have reported a growth in confidence that enables them to participate in staffroom discussions and team meetings in a professional, knowledgeable way. I share Macintyre's experience of students expressing concern over choice of subject matter for research. Often people feel as if they have to find something completely new and different, but this is not so. No two situations are ever the same – the children, conditions, time available, and methods chosen all vary – and besides comparing your situation and results with those of others can be extremely worthwhile. Key features of action research (Macintyre 2000: 7) are that it is

- creative
- contextualised
- realistic
- flexible
- rigorous
- illuminating.

Working as a member of a team

While carrying out a project, one cannot fail to be involved in problem solving that might include risk taking, goal setting, goal sharing, networking and eliciting feedback. The motivation and awareness that result can be of enormous benefit to what becomes a professional team rather than a hierarchical management structure. Each working relationship is unique, based on trust and an understanding and appreciation of the strengths of each team member (Sage and Wilkie, 2003: 12).

Risk taking

Trying something new can be intimidating. This is where having a 'critical friend' can be a powerful key to success. Those who work with you will often be facilitators in terms of allowing access to groups of children, resources, time, etc. Kember (2000: 155) prefers that the facilitator become a supportive collaborator, involved in the project. After all, team members have a stake in the improvement envisaged and need to be encouraged to help shape the work. A third Louise (it is a popular name!) had successfully carried out a project within her foundation class that challenged the gender use of certain activities. This project was successful, as the team members were behind her and actively involved in the aims of her work. Later in her course, Louise tried to initiate improvements in transition between the Foundation stage and Year 1. She planned to create more play-based activities from the learning objectives in Key Stage 1. This was risky, as she was aware that staff in the Key Stage 1 team were not wholly convinced of the benefits of working in this way. Access to suitable accommodation was compromised, and so, therefore, was her inno-vative work. There was a risk that 'latent conflicts and tensions' might be brought into the open (Elliott, 1991: 61). Unfortunately, since the role of the TA is changing and developing, some will feel threatened by TAs who take advantage of opportunities. Some feel that as the definitions of each job become less distinct, the professionalism of teachers, could be eroded (Sage and Wilkie, 2003: 12). It might be viewed as unprofessional to risk disruption of staff relationships, but, on the other hand, some conflict, well handled, can create reappraisal of situations and new motivation. Louise still managed to develop some original and motivating work, but one cannot ignore the part that others play in action research – it is not only your beliefs that you might be challenging.

Goal setting and goal sharing

Consulting the others you work with over your action plan may make time con-straints more feasible, and if they are involved in what you are trying to achieve, deadlines might be easier to meet. Your team members should feel they have a vested interest, that the goals are shared among you. They may be able to think aloud and pose questions that will help with purposeful reviewing of progress. In order to do this, you will need to take into account the wishes of others and respect them. There should be an opportunity for colleagues to review and challenge your findings with regard to fairness, relevance and accu-racy, for example (Hopkins, 2002: 192). Schools should be viewed as professional learning communities, but they have traditionally been seen as 'hierarchical, formal, and bureaucratic' (Cohen et al., 2000: 239), whereas action research is 'collegial, informal, open, collaborative and crosses formal boundaries'. The move toward remodelling the workforce in schools is having an impact on the traditional role of the TA and might make this not such a bar-rier. Hargreaves makes the point that there can be little school development without the development of teachers and vice versa (1994 in Cohen et al.), and I would extend this to the whole staff.

Working with other professionals

Hopkins (2002: 189) advocates the establishing of networks in and out of school to promote staff development and enhance practice. I have seen TAs make such opportunities work to their advantage.

Networking

If you are on a foundation degree course, the opportunities for networking to improve your action research are made for you – you just need to exploit them. Your action research project is likely to occur later in your course, so you will have established some relationships with fellow students. In our case, stu-dents are supervised throughout their research and do not attend university so often, so they can feel isolated. Think of the ways you can build some support.

Perhaps you can start a discussion on a virtual learning environment (VLE). The University of Leicester VLE, Blackboard, has proved a vital source of contact for foundation degree students who are all support staff in schools. Take the initiative and seek out fellow students who are working in a similar context to you even though their project aims are different, or look for people whose project aims are similar but are working in a different context. Sharing ideas, progress notes and so on will be very helpful. Make sure you make the most of occasions when you are asked to share ideas at college: talking together is one of the most valuable ways of learning.

In order to share ideas and enable people to benefit, you could suggest giving a presentation to other TAs on your course but in a different year, perhaps, in your family of schools, or at an LEA meeting for TAs. You have worked hard to find out and express views on a valuable aspect of your work, and people will want to listen. There is a need to work within some kind of infrastructure that is already in place to facilitate this. Chris, whose work I mentioned in Chapter 4, was so successful with her work on ICT supporting learning that she was asked to provide some in-house training for other TAs in her large primary school. This was so successful she is now the TA team leader and organises training opportunities for others. Jo, also previously mentioned regarding her work with dyslexic pupils, thought she was going to speak to just a few members of staff from a nearby school, and found that she was working with the whole staff, but she carried it off beautifully, and then also liaised with other schools about using ICT games to promote learning. Sue has been invited to talk to new foundation degree students during their induction about using mind maps to organise their own study. These kinds of contact to publicise work among peers should be encouraged. One could also share work with audiences, such as parents, and other professionals who come into school, such as community workers.

Eliciting feedback

A crucial feature of the cyclical nature of action research is that progress is reviewed, adapted, and so on. In order to do this, you need to take account of feedback not just while your project is proceeding, but after the initial intervention and after the report has been written. If your work has been submitted for academic assessment, you will have some feedback in this way, but this remains quite discrete. In sharing ideas as in the above section and perhaps in publishing work, you are opening yourself to wider feedback. Some of this may be a little critical or less positive than you hoped. However, if you create a reaction, a debate, this is healthy, and your academic report or published piece should not be the end of the action – it should be a 'slice of life'. There was a before, and there should be an active after as well. Embrace your feedback, consider it rationally and with an open mind, and continue to appraise and reappraise practice.

Action research is an expanding field that commands significant educational attention (Cohen et al., 2000: 241). There are now centres for action research and journals dedicated to the methodology. We should view action research as a vehicle of empowerment for everyone in school and an excellent way for TAs working in education and studying at the same time to contribute to both their academic and professional lives. Working in this way can invigorate relationships with colleagues. Perhaps ideas can be shared during a staff meeting or in-house training day.

It is also important to share news and outcomes from your work with children and with parents, who are major stakeholders in what happens in school. They will be interested to know about change and development. Vehicles for communicating news include assemblies to which parents can be invited, newsletters and the school Website.

Key points

- After all the hard work, your ideas should be shared, especially with the major stakeholders involved.
- To prepare for a viva, make sure you have practised by talking to someone else and that you know your report well.
- Being an active participant in research and reflective practice results in professional growth.
- Taking account of the views held and the support on offer within the team is most important for success in implementing an action-research project.
- Action research makes a difference and is a valid tool for TAs!

Appendices

Responses to the tasks contained in this book are listed chapter by chapter. Some of these contain additional information or points to extend thinking, while others provide feedback and confirmation of the authors' intentions or expectations.

Appendix 2.1 Learn to love Latin!

Academic writing clings firmly to tradition, and scattered throughout texts, you will find odd bits of Latin, that have been adopted as standard expressions and abbreviations, used and understood by all. Here is a brief overview of a few of the more common words and phrases you are likely to meet.

Phrase	Explanation
et al.	'and others': academic texts are often written by several people, so this provides a short way of referring to multiple authors. For example, 'Bigbrayne, Heuge-Swott and Knowlotts' becomes 'Bigbrayne et al.'
ibid. or ib.	'in the same place': this tells you to look back to the last source cited for details about the source
op. cit.	'work cited': this refers you to a source cited earlier in the text, usually before the previous reference
sic	'so' or 'thus': this is usually found written in brackets within or after a direct quotation that contains something odd, unusual, incorrect or questionable, showing that the author is aware that something is not right, but is quoting the original source exactly

Appendix 3.1

The observation sheet I have designed is extremely simple. It has basic information sections to record name, dates and times and could be used to focus on any area that needed to be observed…. . There is a section to enter how long the observation will take and a large section to write what has been observed. I have chosen to use this format because it is easy to complete and will fit in with the observations I do for my action research. The observations I undertake will not be complicated, as I am focusing on an individual child. I will record how often the child needs to rest during a PE session. I will also use the same sheet for the observations I do during two playtime sessions.

TASK 3.1

Sandra completed this activity and produced the proforma shown in Figure 3.7 and commentary.

Child's name:
Year group:
Time observation begins:
Time observation ends:
Focus of observation:
Place of observation:
Observation notes:

Figure 3.7

Appendix 4.1

TASK 4.1

Chris also carried out an observation, this time in a Year 6 class. Numbers in parentheses refer to suggested codes to be found in Figure 4.16.

Throughout the observation, references will be made to children I shall refer to as C and D.

Introduction to lesson – seated in whole-class group on carpet.

C	fidgeting/chatting/facing away from teacher.	(1)
D	staring at display.	(2)

Discussion considered changes to Europe since the First World War

C and D	no involvement in group discussion, no interaction with teacher, as by eye contact/non-verbal gestures.	(1)

As session progressed

D	shows some signs of participation and puts hand up to answer question.	(4)
C	answers question – 'How did Hitler feel?' – inappropriate response.	(4)

Teacher then explained what was required for the lesson – handing out two sheets, a map and an instruction sheet. Teacher asked children to listen carefully. The second sheet told the children exactly what they were going to do. Children asked to look at and read through the sheet.

C and D	seem to be reading sheet.	(4)

Group discussion took place on meaning of terms such as 'allies', 'neutral', etc.

C and D	appear to be interested in map.	(4)

Teacher explained instructions, i.e. in what order, how and in what colour.

C and D	appear to be listening and attempting to read text.	(4)
C and D	chatting.	(1)

Teacher then read the whole sheet to the whole class explaining what was required.

| D | not looking at map, instructions or the teacher. | (1) |
| C | able to contribute to discussion on reading key appropriately. | (4) |

The teacher explained that this was also a test of their ability to follow instructions appropriately. Children returned to their desks to start work on completing sheet. At this time, I checked child's understanding of task.

| C | shows good understanding of what was required. | (4) |
| D | appears to have understanding – however, also states that all cross-hatched should be red. | (4) (2) |

Children commenced activity

D	sharpens pencil.	(1)
C	picks up a red crayon, starts looking around the classroom.	(1)
C and D	look around room – distracted.	(1)
D	initially colours Germany correctly, and then continues to colour all hatched areas red; hand up for help from teacher.	(4) (2) (3)
C	does not complete in order – teacher had explained that this would help with recall.	(2)
D	needs reshowing what he should be copying.	(3)
C and D	teacher reiterates how instructions need to be followed in order so that they would understand how events had unfolded.	(3)
C and D	teacher moves away; both stop working and start a discussion.	(1)
C	tries to support D.	(4)
D	begins playing with pen.	(1)
D	playing with pen.	(1)
C and D	chatting.	(1)
C	starts to work independently when told to finish work before going out for break.	(4)
D	asks to leave room as has pen on face.	(1)

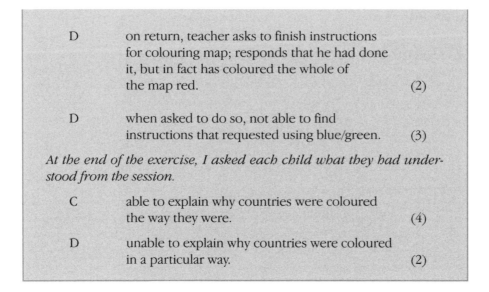

| D | on return, teacher asks to finish instructions for colouring map; responds that he had done it, but in fact has coloured the whole of the map red. | (2) |
| D | when asked to do so, not able to find instructions that requested using blue/green. | (3) |

At the end of the exercise, I asked each child what they had understood from the session.

| C | able to explain why countries were coloured the way they were. | (4) |
| D | unable to explain why countries were coloured in a particular way. | (2) |

Chris chose codes that arose from the observation itself, an example of identifying categories that is referred to as *grounded*, as they originate from the data, not from preconceived objectives. She has grouped, responses, reassembling them where she has seen commonalities between them. Figure 4.16 shows that child D has almost twice as many instances where he displays non-engagement or lack of understanding. It is therefore not surprising that he cannot explain the lesson objectives at the close of the session!

Code	Includes	Child C	Child D
1. Off task	chatting/fidgeting/being distracted	7	10
2. Not participating	no interaction/inappropriate response	2	5
3. Not understanding	needing clarification/remodelling	1	4
	Total	10	19
4. Participating	engaged/interested listening/hand up	9	6

Figure 4.15 completed

Appendix 4.2

TASK 4.2

Reading the data from the photograph (Figure 4.6) might include interpretations such as:

- There is an informal atmosphere – the children are standing, and their work is not formally presented on lines. They have been allowed felt-tip pens.
- They are children of neat appearance – neat hairstyle and school uniform.
- The children seem to be working together and with some autonomy.

Overall, one might conclude that the concept of a school council would be understood and well received by children working in this apparently supportive school and area. Of course, I may just be revealing my own bias! Brown and Dowling (1998: 85) discuss the powerful image of an American soldier, analysing 'readings' in three ways: literal, ironic and neutral. They point out the importance of an 'adequate definition of the empirical setting', and warn that analysis is plausible because it 'addresses interpretive frameworks the reader already possesses'. So you need to know the context and background and be aware of your own knowledge.

Appendix 4.3

TASK 4.3

Comments might include:

- There is a wider diversity of marks when children used bullet points.
- All those who scored less than half-marks liked the mind-map method.
- The only people who gave mind maps a low rating still scored well on the test.

Overall, it appears that students were more successful at the test and keener on the method when using mind maps!

Appendix 5.1

TASK 5.2

Identify the missing information! – checklist

Ainsworth, M.D.S. (1973) 'The development of infant–mother attachment', in B.M. Caldwell and H.N. Ricciuti (eds), *Review of Child Development Research*, vol. 3. Chicago: University of Chicago Press.

Bandura, A. (1973) *Aggression, a Social Learning Analysis*. Englewood Cliffs, NJ: Prentice Hall.

Bee, H. (2000) *The Developing Child* (9th edn). London: Allyn and Bacon.

Bell, N. (1991) *Visualizing and Verbalizing*. Paso Robles, CA: Academy of Reading Publications.

Bell, S.M. (1970) 'The development of the concept of object as related to infant–mother attachment', *Child Development*, 41: 291–311.

Binet, A. and Simon, T. (1916) *The Development of Intelligence in Children*. Baltimore, MD: Williams & Wilkins.

Borke, H. (1975) 'Piaget's mountains revisited: changes in the egocentric landscape', *Developmental Psychology*, 11: 240–3.

Bowlby, J. (1969) *Attachment and Loss*. vol. 1: Attachment. New York: Basic Books.

Brazelton, T.B., Robey, J.S. and Collier, G.A. (1969) 'Infant development in the Zinacanteco Indians of southern Mexico', *Pediatrics*, 44: 274–93.

Bruner, J.S., Olver, R.R. and Greenfield, P.M. (1966) (eds), *Studies in Cognitive Growth*. New York: Wiley.

Cooper, J., Moodley, M. and Reynell, J. (1978) *Helping Language Development*. London: E.A. Arnold.

Cortes, J.B. and Gatti, F.M. (1965) 'Physique and self description of temperament', *Journal of Consulting Psychology*, 20: 432–9.

Dale, P.S. (1976) *Language Development: Structure and Function* (2nd edn). New York: Holt, Rinehart & Winston.

Diorio, D., Viau, V. and Meaney, M.J. (1993) 'The role of the medial prefrontal Cortex in the regulation of hypothalamic-pituitary-adrenal responses to stress', *Journal of Neuroscience*, 13(9): 3839–47.

References

Bartlett, S., Burton, D. and Peim, N. (2001) *Introduction to Education Studies*. London: PCP.

Bassey, M. (1995) *Creating Education Through Research: A Global Perspective of Education Research for the 21st Century*. Newark, NJ: Kirklington Moor Press/BERA.

Bell, J. (1999) *Doing Your Research Project: A Guide for First-Time Researchers in Education and Social Science*. Buckingham: Open University Press.

Blaxter, L., Hughes, C. and Tight, M. (2001) *How to Research*. Buckingham: Open University Press.

Brockbank, A. and McGill, I. (1998) *Facilitating Reflective Learning in Higher Education*. Buckingham: SRHE and Open University Press.

Brockbank, A., McGill, I. and Beech, N. (2002) *Reflective Learning in Practice*. Aldershot: Gower.

Brown, A. and Dowling, P. (1998) *Doing Research/Reading Research*. London: Falmer.

Buzan, T. (1998) *The Mind Map Book*. London: BBC Publications.

Carr, W. and Kemmis, S. (1986) *Becoming Critical; Education Knowledge and Action Research*. Lewes: Falmer.

Cohen, L., Manion, L. and Morrison, K. (2000) *Research Methods in Education*. London: RoutledgeFalmer.

Costello, P. (2003) *Action Research*. London: Continuum.

Cryer, P. (2000) *The Research Student's Guide to Success* (2nd edn). Buckingham: Open University Press.

Drever, E. (1995) *Using Semi-structured Interviews in Small Scale Research: A Teacher's Guide*. Edinburgh: SCRE.

Elliott, J. (1991) *Action Research for Educational Change.* Buckingham: Open University Press.

Farrell, P., Balshaw, M. and Polat, F. (1999) *The Management, Role and Training of Learning Support Assistants*. DfEE: HMSO, Green Paper.

Freebody, P. (2003) *Qualitative Research in Education*. London: Sage.

Freeman, D. (1998) *Doing Teacher Research*. London: Heinle & Heinle.

Gray, D. (2004) *Doing Research in the Real World*. London: Sage.

Haywood, P. and Wragg, E.C. (1978) University of Nottingham School of Education Rediguide 2: *Evaluating the Literature*. Oxford: TRC-Rediguides.

Hopkins, D. (2002) *A Teacher's Guide to Classroom Research* (3rd edn). Maidenhead: Open University Press.

Kember, D. (2000) *Action Learning and Action Research: Improving the quality of teaching and learning*. London: Kogan Page.

Kirk, R. (2002)'Exploring the existing body of research', in M. Coleman and A.R.J. Briggs (eds), *Research Methods in Educational Leadership and Management*. London: Paul Chapman.

Koshy, V. (2005) *Action Research for Improving Practice: A Practical Guide*. London: PCP.

Macintyre, C. (2000) *The Art of Action Research in the Classroom*. London: Fulton.

McBurney, D.H. (1998) *Research Methods* (4th edn). Pacific Grove, CA: Brookes/Cole.

McNiff, J. and Whitehead, J. (2002) *Action Research: Principles and Practice* (2nd edn). London: RoutledgeFalmer.

McNiff, J. and Whitehead, J. (2005) *Action Research for Teachers: A Practical Guide*. London: David Fulton.

Merriam, S. (1988) *Case Study Research in Education*. London: JBL.

Miles, M. and Huberman, M. (1994) *Qualitative Data Analysis*. London: Sage.

Pollard, A. (2002) *Reflective Teaching*. London: Continuum.

Sage, R. and Wilkie, M. (2003) *Supporting Learning in Primary Schools*. Exeter: Learning Matters Ltd.

Sage, R. and Wilkie, M. (2004) *Supporting Learning in Primary Schools* (2nd edn). Exeter: Learning Matters Ltd.

Schon, D.A. (1983) *The Reflective Practitioner*. London: Temple Smith.

Schon, D.A. (1987) *Educating the Reflective Practitioner*. London: Temple Smith.

Warwick, P. (2005) *Developing action-based studies in schools/colleges around foundation subjects*. University of Leicester.

Watkinson, A. (2002) *Assisting Learning and Supporting Teaching*, London: Fulton.

Wragg, E.C. (1999) *An Introduction to Classroom Observation* (2nd edn). London: Routledge.

www.bera.ac.uk

http://bubl.ac.uk August 2005, BUBL Information Service.

www.leeds.ac.uk/bei/bei.htm August 2005, British Education Index.

www.sosig.ac.uk/about_us/what_is.html August 2005, Social Science Information Gateway (SOSIG).

Glossary

Abstract: an overview of a study, presented first.

Active change agent: someone who takes the initiative to effect change in a situation.

ADHD: Attention Deficit Hyperactive Disorder.

Anonymity: the procedure that ensures that names are not made public.

Bias: influence that sways opinion/thinking; imbalance in presentation.

Case study: an approach used to research an aspect of a problem or issue in depth. The resulting data can be rich and highly descriptive, providing an in-depth picture of a particular event, person or phenomenon.

Closed question: one that has a 'set' answer, e.g. 'Yes' or 'No'.

Code: a symbol for 'naming' or grouping data together according to similarities.

Collegial: shared and agreed on by all participants; implies equality.

Confidentiality: a procedure which ensures that information is treated with the strictest confidentiality by the researcher, as agreed with participants.

Correlate: match together evidence from different sources showing complementary or corroboratory aspects.

Disassemble: take apart.

Empirical: based on, or guided by, the results of observation and experiment only.

Ethnography: a style of research originally developed by anthropologists wishing to study cultural groups or aspects of a society in depth. The approach relies heavily upon observation and, in particular, participant observation.

Experimental research: a form of positivist, quantitative research where there is usually a hypothesis that an experiment seeks to prove or disprove.

Generalisability: the degree to which results or inferences drawn from a particular research project can be applied in other situations or circumstances.

Hypothesis: a supposition, theory or provisional explanation to be proved or disproved by exploration of research data.

Interpretivism: a theoretical perspective that argues that the world is interpreted by those engaged with it.

Methodology: explanation of research design – what methods of data collection were chosen and why.

Open question: one that requires a sentence or explanation as a response or that may have several acceptable answers.

Paradigm: a conceptual framework, a perspective.

Participant observation: the act of studying people in their natural settings or 'fields'. As a participant, the researcher becomes part of the group being researched, and understands the situation by experiencing it.

Passive voice: using the third person to attain objectivity or neutrality in writing.

Plagiarism: using the ideas and/or work of somebody else without attributing your source.

Positivism: a theoretical perspective that argues that the properties of the world can be measured through empirical, scientific observation.

Qualitative: the research approach that incorporates an interpretivist perspective.

Qualitative data: evidence exploring the character attributes and/or nature of a situation.

Quantitative: the research approach that incorporates a positivist perspective.

Quantitative data: numerical evidence that can be manipulated and/or presented to explain results.

Reliability: for a data collection method to be reliable, we would expect it to give us the same results whether something was measured today, yesterday, or tomorrow.

Replicate: reproduce research exactly (or as nearly exactly) as possible in order to check, confirm or challenge findings.

Scan: read quickly, looking for particular information.

Significance: the extent to which research findings can be said to have meaning, or consequence, or are worthy of consideration.

Skim: read quickly to ascertain overall sense of a text.

Triangulation: a check for internal consistency, usually made by comparing data from three different sources.

Validity: measures of validity tell us whether a data collection tool actually measures or collects the information it was intended to.

VLE: virtual learning environment – site on the Internet for exclusive use of designated participants to share information and discussion.

Index

Figures are indicated by 'f' following the page number

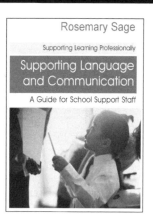